# of HEAVEN & EARTH

500 Years of Italian Painting from Glasgow Museums

Peter Humfrey

Of Heaven and Earth :
500 Years of Italian Painting from Glasgow Museums

Tour Dates

Compton Verney, Warwickshire, England
(as Bellini, Botticelli, Titian... 500 years of Italian Art)

23 March–23 June 2013

www.comptonverney.org.uk

Oklahoma City Museum of Art, Oklahoma, USA

22 August–17 November 2013

www.okcmoa.com

Art Gallery of Alberta, Edmonton, Canada

13 December 2013–9 March 2014

www.youraga.ca

Everson Museum of Art, Syracuse, New York, USA

17 April–13 July 2014

www.everson.org

Milwaukee Art Museum, Wisconsin, USA

3 October 2014–4 January 2015

www.mam.org

Santa Barbara Museum of Art, California, USA
(as Botticelli, Titian and Beyond: Italian Masterpieces from Glasgow Museums)

6 February–3 May 2015

www.sbmuseart.org

Text and images copyright © CSG CIC Glasgow Museums Collection, unless otherwise acknowledged.

First published in 2013 by Glasgow Museums
www.glasgowmuseums.com

ISBN 978-1-908638-02-1

Designed by Alasdair Robertson, Glasgow, Scotland
www.arcimagination.com

Edited by Susan Pacitti

Glasgow Museums photography by Maureen Kinnear and Alan Broadfoot

Printed and bound in Scotland by Allander

Cover printed on Hello Silk 350gsm (FSC Mix Credit – Cert. No. TT-COC-002590; text printed on Hello Silk 170gsm (FSC Mix Credit – Cert. No. TT-COC-002590), using 100% mineral oil-free inks.

MIX
Paper from responsible sources
FSC® C008886

of HEAVEN & EARTH

Contents

Foreword

Foreword

DR ELLEN McADAM

Glasgow owns the finest civic collection in the UK, arguably one of the best civic collections in northern Europe. It is difficult to list the collection areas of international significance without beginning to sound like a Victorian patter song: Old Masters, French Impressionists, Scottish Art, Glasgow Style, natural history, transport and technology, world cultures, Scottish archaeology.... The richness of the collection derives, of course, from the great industrial and mercantile wealth that Glasgow enjoyed in the nineteenth century as the Second City of the Empire and the fourth richest city in Europe, as well as from the generosity and civic pride of her citizens.

For all its distinction, however, Glasgow's collection is not as well known outside the city as it deserves to be. With one or two exceptions, very few areas of the collection have been researched and published, and in order to address this Glasgow Museums created in 2002 the first, and still the only, dedicated research section in any civic museum service in the UK. In keeping with the benevolent intentions of the Victorian city fathers who founded the service, Glasgow Museums has a distinguished record of museum education, public access, outreach and community engagement. However, our knowledge and understanding of the collection, and hence the quality of our interpretive content, has not always kept pace. By encouraging academic research and publication it has been our aspiration to match the commitment to social justice of a local museum service with the excellence of content of a national institution.

Detail from **Virgin and Child,**
c. 1485–88
Giovanni Bellini
Oil on panel
35.4
Gifted as part of the Burrell
Collection to the city of Glasgow,
1944

Detail from **Justice and Peace Embracing**, *c.*1700
Antonio Balestra
Oil on canvas
266
Archibald McLellan Collection, purchased 1856

The publication of Peter Humfrey's complete catalogue of the collection – *Glasgow Museums: The Italian paintings* – to coincide with the opening of the exhibition in Kelvingrove Art Gallery and Museum in April 2012 was a landmark on this journey. This major work of scholarship will be a resource for research for many years to come, and we owe a great debt of gratitude to Professor Humfrey for his immense investment of time and effort. With his knowledge of, and passion for, the collection, there was no one more fitting to be the guest curator for the tour, and the author of this exhibition catalogue.

This tour will bring Glasgow Museums and its collection of Italian paintings to the attention of new audiences, complementing the host venues' own collections and encouraging the appreciation of great art. We hope that in years to come some of these visitors will be inspired to visit Glasgow in person and see our works alongside the rest of our magnificent collection. We are delighted to be associated with Compton Verney as the only other UK venue for this exhibition, and with the American Federation of Arts in bringing these works to a North American audience. Both organizations have worked hard and enthusiastically to develop this tour, and we look forward to continuing our partnerships with them on future projects.

We would like to thank the Friends of Glasgow Museums and Museums Galleries Scotland for their support in researching and conserving these works.

Dr Ellen McAdam
Head of Museums and Collections, Glasgow Museums

Acknowledgements

AMERICAN FEDERATION OF ARTS

With works by some of the greatest names in European art, Glasgow Museums is home to an extraordinary collection of Italian paintings. Only a small portion of these have been displayed in recent years, however, and most of those in *Of Heaven and Earth* have never before been shown outside Glasgow. It is therefore a particular pleasure for the American Federation of Arts to have co-organized this exhibition with Glasgow Museums and thus be able to bring greater recognition to a selection of these celebrated and sumptuous works. I am proud to add that this marks the second collaboration between the AFA and Glasgow Museums. In 2002, the two institutions co-organized *Millet to Matisse: Nineteenth- and Twentieth-Century French Painting from Kelvingrove Art Gallery, Glasgow.*

First and foremost our gratitude goes to Ellen McAdam, Head of Museums and Collections at Glasgow Museums/Glasgow Life, and the rest of her staff for being such collegial partners. We are also enormously indebted to our guest curator, Peter Humfrey, whose expertise in the field of Italian art history is renowned. We thank Peter particularly for his publication text, which is characterized by his customary meticulous scholarship.

The staff of the AFA deserve recognition for their superb work on behalf of this project. I wish to acknowledge Anna Evenhouse, Associate Director for Exhibitions; Michelle Hargrave, Curator of Exhibitions; Jennifer Hefner, Senior Registrar; Alice Hunsberger, Associate Director for Development; Suky Kang, Curatorial Assistant; and Juliet Helmke, Publications Assistant; as well as former Associate Director for Publications and Communications Michaelyn Mitchell, and former Curatorial Assistant Luke Baker.

The exhibition tour is generously supported by the JFM Foundation and the Donald and Maria Cox Charitable Fund. We extend our deep gratitude to Barbara and Richard S. Lane and Christie's for their in-kind support.

Finally, we recognize the museums presenting this important exhibition – the Oklahoma City Museum of Art, the Art Gallery of Alberta, Edmonton, Canada, the Everson Museum of Art, Syracuse, NY, the Milwaukee Art Museum, and the Santa Barbara Museum of Art. Working with them has been a pleasure.

Pauline Willis   *Director*, American Federation of Arts

Detail from **St John the Baptist Revealing Christ to the Disciples**, 1656–57

Salvator Rosa
Oil on canvas
Signed: SR
2969
Presented to Glasgow Museums in memory of John Young by his family, 1952

Acknowledgements

COMPTON VERNEY

We are delighted to be working in partnership with Glasgow Museums as the only other UK venue for this spectacular and important exhibition, and would like to extend our huge thanks to Ellen McAdam and her team for the opportunity to collaborate and for the support they have given us over the past two years. Compton Verney has a proud history of bringing artworks of the highest quality to the South Midlands, and this exhibition will add a fresh new dimension to our own, unique collection of Neapolitan paintings.

Dr Steven Parissien

Director, Compton Verney, Warwickshire, England

Detail from **Landscape with St Jerome,** *c.*1610
Domenichino
Oil on panel
139
Archibald McLellan Collection, purchased 1856

Glasgow's Collections

Glasgow's Collections

DR MARTIN BELLAMY

Glasgow City Council owns one of the finest museum collections in Europe, consisting of approximately one million objects cared for on its behalf by Glasgow Museums, the museums division of Glasgow Life. These encompass a broad spectrum of art and design, human history, natural history and transport and technology. The art collection is recognized as one of the best in the UK, and covers a wide range of media including paintings, drawings, prints, sculpture, metalwork, ceramics, glass, jewellery, furniture and textiles. It provides a comprehensive overview of the history of European art and design, with masterpieces by major artists such as Rembrandt, Van Gogh, Whistler and Dali. Works from non-European cultures include an internationally renowned collection of Chinese art (fig. 1).

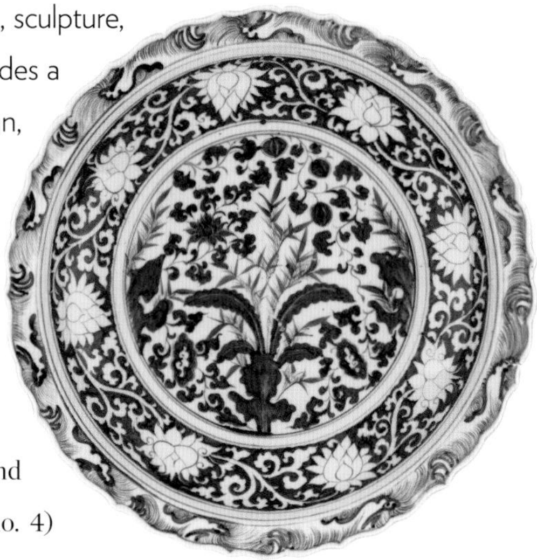

The development of the art collection began with the 1854 bequest of 510 paintings by Glasgow coachbuilder Archibald McLellan (1795–1854). He was a prolific collector of Italian, Dutch and Flemish art, and his gift included gems such as Botticelli's *The Annunciation* (cat. no. 4) and Titian's *Christ and the Adulteress* (cat. no. 9). Unfortunately McLellan was insolvent at the time of his death, and there were numerous claims on his property by his creditors. Before the City could acquire the collection, it had to pay off his debts, and it was only after more than a year of debate and a narrow vote in Council that the collection was acquired. One of those who argued strongly for the acquisition was the philanthropist and collector William Euing (1788–1874), who donated 30 paintings

Fig. 1
Porcelain dish, Yuan dynasty
Jingdezhen, China
Porcelain
38.658
Gifted as part of the Burrell Collection to the city of Glasgow, 1944

Detail from **The Druids – Bringing in the Mistletoe,** 1890
George Henry and Edward Atkinson Hornel
Oil on canvas
1534
Purchased by Glasgow Museums, 1922

Opposite Fig. 2
A Man in Armour, possibly 1655
Harmensz van Rijn Rembrandt
Oil on canvas
601
Bequest of Mrs John Graham Gilbert, 1877

from his own collection shortly after McLellan's collection was accepted. He later bequeathed the remainder of his collection of some 200 works to the City.

Another major acquisition came in 1877, when Jane Graham Gilbert, widow of the portrait painter John Graham Gilbert (1794–1866), died and bequeathed her husband's collection and all his unfinished works. Among the 70 works are copies of Italian paintings made during his training, as well as Italian and Dutch Old Masters, including Rembrandt's *Man in Armour* (fig. 2), one of the greatest works in the collection.

Fig. 3
Interior of McLellan Galleries Central Hall, *c.* 1860

Mark Dessurne
Watercolour
TEMP.7582.4
Glasgow Museums

Fig. 4
**The Blute-Fin Windmill,
Montmartre,** 1886

Vincent van Gogh
Oil on canvas
2425
Bequest of William McInnes, 1944

While the collection itself was growing and improving, the gallery in which it was displayed was becoming something of an embarrassment to the City. Archibald McLellan's partially completed gallery (fig. 3) was acquired along with his collection and was used as the Corporation's art gallery. In order to recoup expenses it was hired out for balls and soirées, and the physical damage incurred during these gatherings was compounded by poor ventilation, dirty gas lighting and a lack of maintenance. By the late nineteenth century, Glasgow had become one of the principal manufacturing and commercial centres in the country and was styling itself as the Second City of the Empire. In order to reflect this status, the City decided to create a new combined museum and art gallery, which, in the words of the Convener of the Museums and Galleries Committee, was 'adequate for the necessities and dignity of the great commercial and industrial city of Glasgow'. In 1888, the city's first International Exhibition was held expressly to raise funds for the new museum. This was followed in 1901 with a second International Exhibition, to celebrate the newly constructed Kelvingrove Art Gallery and Museum and to raise funds for future acquisitions.

Glasgow's massive expansion in the late nineteenth century saw the rise of an industrial elite who developed a taste for collecting art. Many were extremely discerning and knowledgeable, and their gifts now form the backbone of the collection. Their motivations for giving were a mix of status aggrandizement, civic pride and philanthropy, but most adhered to McLellan's belief that 'the study of what are called the "fine arts" is eminently conducive to the elevation and refinement of all classes, as well as intimately connected with the manufacturing and mercantile prosperity of this community'. Among the industrialist collectors who donated paintings are the shipbuilder Isabella Elder, the chemical manufacturer William Chrystal and the engineer Sir John Richmond.

Dr Tom Honeyman, director of the Museums Service from 1939 to 1954, was highly influential in encouraging industrialist collectors to donate to the city. He courted

Fig. 5

The Château de Medan, c.1879–80

Paul Cézanne

Oil on canvas

35.53

Gifted as part of the Burrell Collection to the city of Glasgow, 1944

William McInnes, a shipping company owner with a particular fondness for French art, for many years. His bequest in 1944 of over 70 paintings included Monet's *Vétheuil*, Van Gogh's *The Blute-Fin Windmill, Montmartre* (fig. 4) and Picasso's *The Flower Seller*.

However, the greatest gift came from shipping magnate Sir William Burrell (1861–1958). His collection of nearly 9,000 objects covers a vast array of works from every period from all over the world, including important medieval tapestries, stained glass,

English oak furniture, European paintings and sculpture, and important collections of Chinese and Islamic art. Significant paintings in his collection include Rembrandt's *Self Portrait*, Degas' *The Rehearsal*, and Cézanne's *The Château de Medan* (fig. 5). One of the remarkable strengths of Burrell's collection is that he deliberately purchased groups of works by specific artists including Géricault, Millet, Daumier, Courbet, Manet and Degas.

As well as receiving gifts from private collectors, Glasgow Museums has been very active in purchasing art. The most high profile acquisition is undoubtedly Salvador Dali's *Christ of St John of the Cross* (fig. 6). This was an inspired purchase by Dr Tom Honeyman, a friend of Dali's, who managed to secure the work despite major opposition in the Council and from students at the Glasgow School of Art. However, it received major public acclaim and has remained one of the most iconic and loved paintings in Glasgow's collection. The Dali was purchased from the remainder of the 1901 Exhibition purchase fund, but other major acquisitions have been made possible using funds from the Hamilton Bequest, which derives from the combined estates of the storekeeper John Hamilton and his two sisters, Elizabeth and Christina. They gave a sum of money in 1927 solely for the purchase of oil paintings for Kelvingrove. The fund is still administered by the Hamilton Trustees, and has presented some 80 paintings including Rossetti's *Regina Cordium: Alice Wilding*, Gauguin's *Østre Anlæg Park, Copenhagen* and Monet's *View of Ventimiglia*. Thus, with a combination of generous gifts and judicious purchasing, Glasgow Museums has established an internationally significant art collection with major strengths in European and Scottish art.

Fig. 6
Christ of St John of the Cross,
1951

Salvador Dali

Oil on canvas

2964

Purchased by Glasgow Museums,
1952

As described elsewhere in this catalogue in greater detail, the collection of Italian paintings is among the finest, both intellectually and aesthetically, held by any municipal museums service in the UK. It includes works dating from the fourteenth to the late nineteenth century originating from the main artistic centres of Italy such as Venice, Bologna, Rome, Florence and Naples. A number of important fifteenth- and sixteenth-century Venetian School works by major artists such as Giovanni Bellini, Titian, and Paris Bordon form the backbone of the collection. It also includes paintings closely associated with the workshops of Botticelli, Lippi and Pesellino, and boasts seventeenth- and eighteenth-century works of particularly high quality and importance by Carlo Dolci, Domenichino, Francesco Guardi and Salvator Rosa.

The Spanish collection is the second largest in the UK. The majority of the paintings date from the late sixteenth and seventeenth centuries, and include works by El Greco, Cano, Velazquez (workshop), Ribera (workshop) and Murillo. Later works include paintings by Goya, Juan Gris and Salvador Dali. The collection of Spanish paintings is of particular historical interest, having been formed largely by the pioneering local collector William Stirling Maxwell (1818–1878). The substantial group of Habsburg portraits, which reflects Stirling Maxwell's preoccupation with the history of Spain, is the finest outside Madrid and Vienna.

The Dutch and Flemish collection is of unusual depth and breadth and is among the largest in the world outside the great national or princely collections. It includes paintings, watercolours and gouaches made between c.1450 and c.1960. Dutch art

Fig. 7
The Virgin and Child by a Fountain, 1515–41
Bernard van Orley
Oil on panel
201
Archibald McLellan Collection, purchased 1856

forms the largest part of this collection. Old Masters include Rembrandt, de Lairesse, and Rubens. Later works include a significant collection of nineteenth-century Hague School paintings. The majority of the works from the southern Netherlands date from the seventeenth century, and the collection includes the fine *The Virgin and Child by a Fountain* (fig. 7) by Bernard van Orley.

The collection of French nineteenth-century oils is one of the largest, finest and most important in the United Kingdom. It covers some of the key artistic movements of this time, with stunning individual masterpieces and works by many of the most important French artists working in the period 1800–1950. The collection ranges from early nineteenth-century works by Théodore Géricault to paintings by Georges Braque and Henri Matisse from the early twentieth century. It covers a wide range of styles, including the Barbizon School, Impressionism, Post-Impressionism and Fauvism.

Opposite Fig. 8
Arrangement in Grey and Black, No. 2: Thomas Carlyle, 1872–73
James Abbott McNeill Whistler
Oil on canvas
671
Purchased by Glasgow Museums, 1891

The British collection includes some outstanding individual masterpieces by key artists. Most of the works are of high artistic quality, and the collection as a whole provides a substantial contribution towards an overview of British art. Among the more significant works are Turner's *Modern Italy – the Pifferari* and Whistler's internationally important *Arrangement in Grey and Black No. 2 : Thomas Carlyle* (fig. 8), the first painting by the artist to enter a public collection.

Fig. 9
The Cuillin from Ord, Skye,
c.1854

Horatio McCulloch
Oil on canvas
1052
Gifted by Archibald G Macdonald,
1896

The Scottish collection is one of the most comprehensive in the country, being especially rich in nineteenth- and twentieth-century painting. It includes works by many of the key figures in Scottish art, including Henry Raeburn, Horatio McCulloch (fig. 9), William McTaggart and Joan Eardley. It includes eighteenth- and nineteenth-century portraits, eighteenth- and nineteenth-century landscapes, and Scottish Victorian narrative and history paintings.

The collection of works by the Glasgow Boys is of great significance, and the overall aesthetic quality of the works extremely high. The most significant areas of the collection include an excellent group of 'rustic realist' pictures painted in the early 1880s by Guthrie, Paterson and Kennedy, including Guthrie's *Old Willie* and *A Funeral Service in the Highlands*. The group of 'Symbolist' pictures from the 1890s includes *The Druids – Bringing in the Mistletoe* (fig. 10), a joint collaboration by Henry and Hornel.

Fig. 10

The Druids – Bringing in the Mistletoe, 1890

George Henry and Edward Atkinson Hornel

Oil on canvas

1534

Purchased by Glasgow Museums, 1922

The breadth of the collection is such that many lesser-known Glasgow Boy artists are also represented by significant works in their careers.

The collection of Scottish Colourists also has excellent breadth and depth, and includes a fine group of early landscapes painted in Scotland and France by Fergusson and Peploe; a series of mature landscapes mainly of Scottish views by Peploe, Cadell and Hunter; a group of Cadell 'ladies in interiors'; an excellent group of Peploe still-lifes; and some strong figurative compositions painted in Paris by Fergusson.

More recent Scottish artists such as John Bellany and John Byrne are also well represented in the collection. Their work paved the way for a renewed interest in figurative and narrative painting exemplified by the New Glasgow Boys – Peter Howson, Ken Currie, Adrian Wiszniewski and Steven Campbell. The collection contains some rare and unique examples of their work, including Currie's monumental and eerie *The Bathers* (fig. 11) and Howson's popular *The Glorious Game*. Glasgow has established its reputation as an international centre for contemporary visual arts, and the collection contains a number of important works by Glasgow-based artists who have become internationally significant, including a number of Turner Prize-winners.

As with most municipal collections, some works are important for their high artistic merit, while others are important because their subject matter provides an important historical record of local people and places. Glasgow Life, the operating name for Culture and Sport Glasgow, is responsible for nine museums across the city of Glasgow.

The principal museums in which the collection is displayed are Kelvingrove Art Gallery and Museum, which has comprehensive displays of the major Scottish and European paintings, the Burrell Collection, where Sir William Burrell's collection can be seen, and the Gallery of Modern Art, which displays elements of the permanent collection alongside temporary exhibitions. Paintings of a local character can be seen at the People's Palace, which has an important early commission from Ken Currie. Glasgow's Spanish paintings can still be seen in Pollok House, the former home of William Stirling Maxwell, now run on the City's behalf by the National Trust for Scotland. Paintings not on display can be accessed at Glasgow Museums Resource Centre, which now houses one of the largest painting stores in Europe.

Dr Martin Bellamy
Research and Curatorial Manager, Glasgow Museums

Fig. 11
The Bathers, 1992–93
Ken Currie
Oil on linen
3525
Purchased by Glasgow Museums, 1993

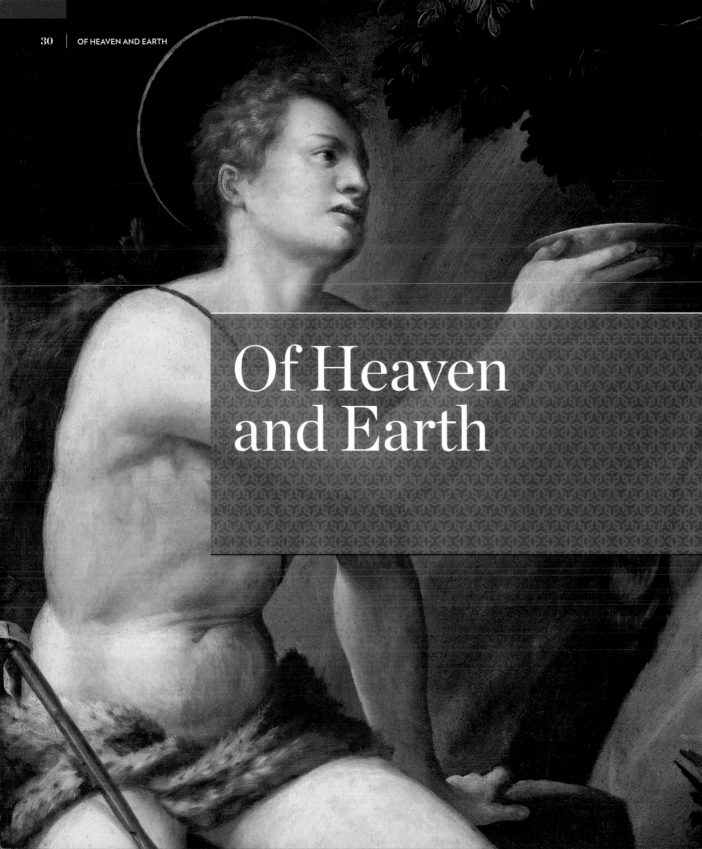

Of Heaven and Earth

500 Years of Italian Painting from Glasgow Museums

PROFESSOR PETER HUMFREY

Glasgow Museums has the fortune to own what is probably the finest and most comprehensive collection of Italian paintings of any civic museums service in Britain. Numbering about 150 paintings, and today housed in several buildings, including Kelvingrove Museum and Art Gallery, the Burrell Collection, Pollok House, and Glasgow Museums Resource Centre, the collection is remarkable both for the quality and interest of individual works and for its chronological range. The 41 works included in this exhibition have been selected to do justice to both these aspects of the collection. Some of Glasgow's finest Italian pictures are unfortunately unable to travel: the beautiful tondo by the fifteenth-century Florentine painter Raffaellino del Garbo (fig. 12), for example, is physically too fragile; and the paintings from the Burrell Collection, including a *Virgin and Child* by Giovanni Bellini (fig. 13), are prevented by the terms of the donor's bequest from leaving the United Kingdom. But present in the exhibition are a number of unquestionable masterpieces, including Signorelli's *Lamentation* (cat. no. 3), another *Virgin and Child* by Bellini (cat. no. 5), Domenichino's *St Jerome in the Desert* (cat. no. 16), a pair of monumental landscapes by Salvator Rosa (cat. nos. 19, 20), Francesco Guardi's *View of San Giorgio Maggiore* (cat. no. 33), and perhaps most celebrated of all, Titian's *Christ and the Adulteress* (cat. no. 9). Chronologically, the exhibition extends from Niccolò di Buonaccorso's *St Lawrence* of c.1375 (cat. no. 1) to Luigi da Rios's *Overlooking a Canal, Venice* (cat. no. 40), painted 500 years later.

Detail from **St John the Baptist in the Wilderness,** c. 1570–75

Florentine, later 16th century
Oil on panel
1588
Bequeathed by Sir Claude Phillips, 1924

Fig. 12
**Virgin and Child
with the Child Baptist
and Two Angels,** *c.* 1493–94

Raffaellino del Garbo

Tempera on circular panel

1015

Given by Mrs Mary Ann Walker in
memory of her father, James Young,
1902

Fig. 13
Virgin and Child, c. 1485–88

Giovanni Bellini

Oil on panel

35.4

Gifted as part of the Burrell
Collection to the city of Glasgow,
1944

Fig. 14
Archibald McLellan, 1906

Robert Cree Crawford,
after John Graham Gilbert

Oil on canvas

1191

Glasgow Museums

Fig. 15
Exterior view of the McLellan Galleries, Sauchiehall Street, Glasgow, 1857

All five centuries are represented by high-quality paintings that reflect the constant stylistic inventiveness of Italian art in a range of different creative centres, from Venice and Bologna to Florence and Naples. And although a majority are religious in theme, they also show a representative range of secular subjects, from ancient history, mythology and allegory, to genre, landscape and townscape.

About one half of the paintings in the present exhibition belonged to Archibald McLellan (1797–1854) (fig. 14), whose private collection formed the nucleus of what was to become Glasgow's civic collection. A coachbuilder by profession, McLellan rose rapidly in the civic hierarchy of the booming mercantile city, serving as magistrate, Deacon of the Trades' Hall, and Bailie on the Town Council. A full-length portrait painted in 1834 by John Graham Gilbert provides an eloquent testimony to the civic dignity that he had attained by this date. He was also closely involved in a number of schemes of public utility and philanthropy, and was highly active in the promotion of the visual arts in the city. At the time of his premature death in 1854, however, he was deeply in debt, having over-reached himself in the development of property in the principal thoroughfare of Glasgow's fashionable west end, Sauchiehall Street, where he intended to provide permanent accommodation for his collection of paintings (fig. 15).

In contrast with what is known about his public offices and financial affairs, very little information survives about McLellan's private life. Particularly disappointing is the almost complete absence of surviving documentation relating to his purchases of paintings. It is known that he never went to Italy, or indeed anywhere beyond the shores of Britain; indeed, before the opening of the first direct train link between Glasgow and London in 1849 (a journey of about 400 miles), he is unlikely to have been a frequent visitor to sales at London auction houses such as Christie's. He seems rather to have used trusted dealers as intermediaries; and as has recently been discovered, between 1839 and 1846 he bought some 13 Italian pictures from John Smith of Bond Street, London, including the Sammacchini in the present exhibition (cat. no. 13).

While it is difficult to give an adequate account of the motives that fired McLellan as a collector, or of how his tastes evolved, some idea of his priorities may be inferred from the paintings themselves. Further, there exists one document of prime importance for understanding McLellan's philosophy of collecting. This is the Deed of Bequest that he included in his will of 1853, which reads:

I, Archibald M'Lellan, coachbuilder in Glasgow, considering that I have, for thirty years spent much of my spare time in making a collection of pictures, illustrative of the characteristics and progress of the various schools of painting in Italy, Germany, Spain, the Low Countries, and France, since the revival of art in the fifteenth century; and believing that, imperfect as any such collection formed by a private individual must necessarily be, it still may be of some use to those who are desirous of studying the progress of art; and also believing that it may be made to form the foundation for a more extensive and complete collection, through contributions from those who have more means and better judgment to select fine examples of the respective schools; and being impressed with the belief that the study of what are called the 'Fine Arts' is eminently conducive to the elevation and refinement of all classes, as well as intimately connected with the manufacturing and mercantile prosperity of this community, – from these various motives, and on account of my long connection with Glasgow and its various public bodies, and as a humble testimony of my attachment to its citizens, and my desire for their welfare and elevation, so far as it is in my power to aid in the promotion of these, I have resolved to devote my said collection to public use and exhibition, and to make the same over, for that purpose, to trustees, who shall have the sole control and management thereof.

The allusion to 'thirty years' in the first line dates the beginning of McLellan's activity as a collector to the early 1820s. This was a golden moment for art-collecting in Britain, as paintings from the former aristocratic and ecclesiastical collections of France and Italy flooded on to the London art market in the peace that followed the downfall of Napoleon. McLellan would have been quite young, still in his twenties, when he began collecting, but it is probable that his picture-buying activity accelerated as time went on, perhaps reaching a climax in the 1840s. Presumably it began as a pleasurable hobby, imitating, albeit on a more modest scale, the activities of the 10th Duke of Hamilton (1767–1852), whose magnificent collection at nearby Hamilton Palace McLellan would certainly have known. Hardly surprisingly, his purchases of Italian pictures conform to much the same taste as that of his socially more privileged, and also better educated, neighbours. In the decades before John Ruskin (1819–1900) and others raised the profile of the so-called Primitives – the painters of the fourteenth and fifteenth centuries – the most admired phases of Italian painting were the first halves of the sixteenth and the seventeenth centuries, with general approval extended to the whole period from about the late fifteenth to the late eighteenth centuries. It is symptomatic of McLellan's apparently rather conventional taste that none of his Italian pictures date from before the 1490s; nor does his collection reflect any interest in Italian art of his own century. His fine examples of Venetian painting of the mid Settecento by such painters as Francesco Zuccarelli (cat. no. 34) and Francesco Guardi (cat. no. 33) probably represented for him the end of a great tradition.

At some point in his career as a collector – especially, perhaps, as he became more confirmed in his life as a bachelor – the idea of eventually bequeathing his collection to his native city must have taken root in his mind. Long before he drew up his Deed of Bequest, his conception of the purpose of his collection must also have evolved from one simply of personal enjoyment to one that reflected the moral and educational aims expressed in the document. From his own words, it is clear that McLellan shared a belief widespread in the early and mid Victorian period that the exposure of the working classes to art could have a direct and beneficial influence on the standards of their behaviour; and in a city where the numbers of urban poor were multiplying daily, the governing classes had a particular responsibility for the improvement of public morality, including through the establishment of a civic art collection. Since education played an important part in this task, it was important that such a collection should not be formed according to personal whim, but should be designed along art-historical lines, to reflect the development of the different national schools of painting, and within Italy, of the different regional schools. In his aspiration to form 'a Collection of Pictures illustrative of the characteristics and progress of the various schools of painting' McLellan was clearly influenced by the museological philosophy of leading contemporary experts such as Gustav Friedrich Waagen (1794–1868), Director of the Berlin Museum, and Charles Eastlake (1793–1865), Keeper at the National Gallery, London. With this aim, McLellan must at some point have adopted a more systematic approach to his activity as a collector, guided as much by the need to fill historical gaps as by a pursuit of quality. He sought to acquire works by some of the most admired of the Italian masters; and when these were not available, he aimed to have them represented by good copies. Like Waagen, he would have regarded it as essential for any self-respecting public gallery to have the Italian, as well as the Netherlandish, School numerically well represented, since these two schools developed earlier than the French, Spanish or British, and hence were of superior historical importance.

McLellan's pursuit, at least by the 1840s, of principles of collecting more usually associated with a national gallery than with a regional museum or a private collection, had further implications for his choice of acquisitions. In contrast to other middle-class buyers of his generation, who typically show a preference for portraiture, landscape and genre, it is noticeable that McLellan – at least with regard to Italian painting – deliberately sought out works with elevated, historical subjects. The great majority of his Italian pictures are religious or mythological in content, and were clearly acquired in the spirit of an academic ideal rather than for any personal or sentimental reasons. Himself a member of the (Presbyterian) Church of Scotland, he did not allow the prejudices of his still overwhelmingly Protestant compatriots to prevent him buying pictures that displayed an overtly Catholic religiosity, such as the *Virgin and Child* by Solimena included here (cat. no. 27). Similarly, the acquisition of overtly sensual pictures, such as Francesco del Cairo's *Death of Cleopatra* (cat. no. 23) or Andrea Casali's *Triumph of Galatea* (cat. no. 30), displays a broad-mindedness that is perhaps surprising for an early Victorian pillar of his community.

By the 1840s McLellan owned one of the most important non-aristocratic private collections in Britain. It was famous enough for Dr Waagen himself to make a point of visiting it in 1851 on the first of his two trips to Scotland; and although Waagen observed that 'the taste for collecting has at present little obtained among rich merchants and manufacturers in Glasgow', he found that McLellan 'forms an honourable exception', describing him as 'a most ardent lover of the arts'. The works selected by Waagen for comment were mainly Flemish and Dutch, but he also recorded 12 of the Italian pictures, including those by Paris Bordon (cat. no. 11), the Cavaliere d'Arpino (cat. no. 15), and Domenichino (cat. no. 16).

When McLellan died in 1854 the bequest of his collection to the city of Glasgow was at first the cause of acute embarrassment for the Town Council. To accept it was also to accept responsibility for the late donor's considerable debts; and even when these were discharged, the collection would still have to be housed at public expense. Several of the city's councillors were, in any case, distinctly unenthusiastic about McLellan's pictures, one dismissing it as a 'collection of rubbish', and another decrying the displays of nudity. The testimony of expert witnesses, however, including Eastlake and the dealer John Smith, was quoted as evidence of the aesthetic and monetary value of the collection; and thanks especially to the energy of the Lord Provost, Andrew Orr, the Council was persuaded at its meeting on 10 April 1856 to purchase the McLellan buildings in Sauchiehall Street and the picture collection at a combined knockdown price of £44,500.

One of the early visitors to the collection in its new home was Waagen, in the course of his second journey to Scotland in 1856. He noted with approval that 'the patriotic feeling which induced the late Mr McLellan to bequeath his collection of pictures to the city of Glasgow has been worthily recognized by the erection of a building, containing three noble and well-lighted apartments in which the pictures are seen by the public'. Coming from Germany, with its multiplicity of local capitals, Waagen was very keen to support the foundation of regional art galleries in the big cities outside London, because of their perceived educational benefit for the populace at large. For the same reason he applauded the temporary loan by the Earl of Elgin of several of his pictures to Glasgow Museums, 'so that they might be generally seen'. He now listed 12 more Italian pictures, not recorded on his previous visit, including Titian's *Christ and the Adulteress* (the high art-historical importance of which he recognized, but which he attributed to Giorgione) (cat. no. 9), Botticelli's *Annunciation* (cat. no. 4), and Guardi's *View of San Giorgio Maggiore* (cat. no. 33).

Fig. 16
John Graham Gilbert, 1870
William Brodie
Marble
S.40
Bequest of Mrs John Graham Gilbert, 1877

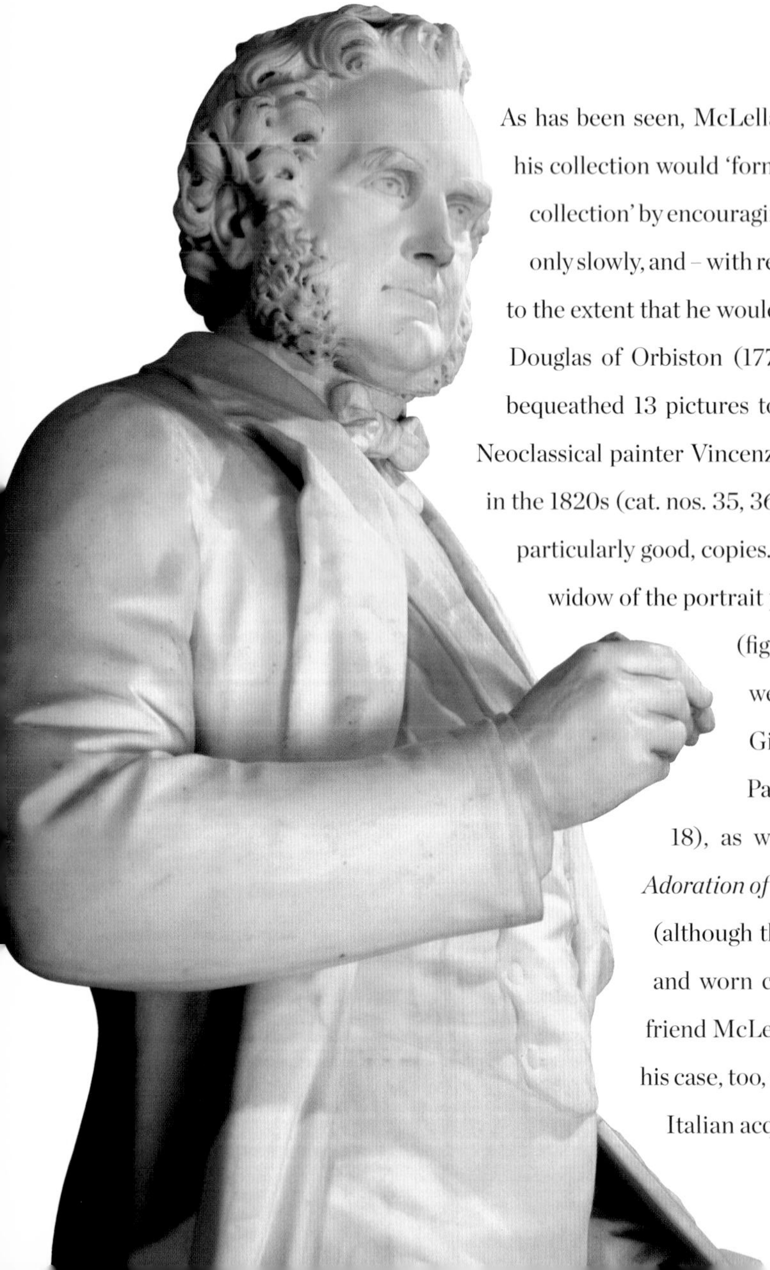

As has been seen, McLellan expressed the hope in his Deed of Bequest that his collection would 'form the foundation for a more extensive and complete collection' by encouraging further bequests. This hope, however, was realized only slowly, and – with respect to the Italian pictures, at least – probably never to the extent that he would have wished. In 1862 the very wealthy Mrs Cecilia Douglas of Orbiston (1771–1862), who had lived for many years in Rome, bequeathed 13 pictures to Glasgow Museums, including two by the leading Neoclassical painter Vincenzo Camuccini, which she had herself commissioned in the 1820s (cat. nos. 35, 36), but most of the others of which were modern, not particularly good, copies. The next important bequest came in 1877, from the widow of the portrait painter John Graham Gilbert, who had died in 1866 (fig. 16). Although only 12 of the 138 items in the bequest were Italian, several of these, including pictures by Giovanni Bellini (cat. no. 5), Palma Vecchio (fig. 17), Paris Bordon (cat. no. 10) and Sassoferrato (cat. no. 18), as well as by the anonymous Master of the Glasgow *Adoration of the Magi* (cat. no. 8), are of great quality and interest (although the Palma is unfortunately in a structurally unstable and worn condition). Graham Gilbert was close in age to his friend McLellan, and his taste in pictures was broadly similar. In his case, too, regrettably little is known of the circumstances of his Italian acquisitions.

The implementation of the Graham Gilbert bequest in 1877 had the positive effect of making the Town Council take its art collection more seriously than it had done since the death of McLellan, and in 1881 it commissioned a report from JC (later Sir Charles) Robinson (1824–1913), the Queen's Surveyor of Pictures, with the aim of identifying the outstanding masterpieces. Of the approximately 120 works singled out for particular praise by Robinson were nine Italian pictures, with the *Christ and the Adulteress* in prime position. Two years later Robinson succeeded in persuading the Provost and his Councillors to make a rare and excellent purchase: Carlo Dolci's *Salome*, formerly in the Stourhead collection (cat. no. 22).

Fig. 17

Virgin and Child with Saints John the Baptist, Peter, and a Female Saint, c. 1523–26

Palma Vecchio

Oil on panel

585

Bequeathed by Mrs John Graham Gilbert, 1877

Fig. 18
Kelvingrove Art Gallery and
Museum, Glasgow, Scotland.

By this time, the accommodation provided by the McLellan Galleries had become seriously inadequate, and in his report Robinson urged the Provost to provide 'a safer and more worthy housing of the treasures in your keeping'. It was decided to construct a museum building that would combine the function of the Art Galleries in Sauchiehall Street with that of the existing City Industrial Museum in Kelvingrove Park, and the essential funding for this ambitious project was provided by an international exhibition held in 1888, under the title of the First Glasgow International Exhibition of Science and Art. A competition for the design of the new building was held in 1892, and a Second International Exhibition was held in the surrounding park to coincide with the completion of the new Kelvingrove Museum in 1901 (fig. 18). In October 1902 all 850 paintings in the civic collection were put on display in the upper-floor galleries.

A few sporadic gifts of Italian pictures also took place while the new museum was under construction during the later 1890s, including Garzi's *Sacrifice of Marcus Curtius*,

bequeathed by William Kennedy in 1899 (cat. no. 26); and among the 117 modern paintings left to Glasgow Museums by the wine merchant Adam Teacher (1838/9–98) were the first four works by living Italian painters to reach the civic collection, including Da Rios's *Overlooking a Canal* of 1886 (cat. no. 40). Even more important than these was the presentation in 1900 and 1902 of a group of pictures that had previously belonged to the eminent chemist and industrialist James Young (1811–1883) (fig. 19) by two

Fig. 19
James Young
John Watson Gordon
Lithograph
TEMP.19243
Glasgow Museums

of his children. James 'Paraffin' Young – so-called because of his development of the paraffin lamp, among other industrial and domestic products – had spent his retirement building up an important collection of paintings at his home at Kelly, Renfrewshire; and among the works that now came to Glasgow Museums was the tondo by Raffaellino del Garbo (acquired as a Botticelli, and later also attributed to Filippino Lippi) (fig. 12). Young also acquired from Florence two magnificent landscapes with scenes from the life of John the Baptist by Salvator Rosa (cat. nos. 19, 20), but in their case Glasgow Museums had to wait for another half century before it received them from a younger generation of Young's descendants.

From now on, however, despite the existence of the grandiose new building, Glasgow Museums was to receive rather few important gifts of Italian pictures. The most significant bequest of the inter-war years consisted, in fact, of the three small, but choice, sixteenth-century works by Girolamo da Carpi (cat. no. 12), Paolo Fiammingo and an anonymous Florentine (cat. no. 14), left to Glasgow Museums by Sir Claude Phillips

(1846–1924). Phillips, the first Keeper of the Wallace Collection, London, and a leading figure in the art establishment of late Victorian and Edwardian London, owned an impressive collection, but left most of it to the National Gallery, London, and shared out what he considered to be its lesser pieces among a number of regional museums, including the National Gallery of Scotland, Edinburgh, and Glasgow Museums.

In the period after World War II the City of Glasgow received as gifts two collections of quite outstanding importance: the Burrell collection in 1944, and the Stirling Maxwell collection in 1967. The former, put together by the ship-owning magnate Sir William Burrell (1861–1958), consists of some 8,000 objects from an exceptionally wide range of cultures. On the whole, however, Burrell did not share the traditional interest in the central canon of European painting, including Italian, and his acquisition in 1936 of a masterpiece by Giovanni Bellini (fig. 2) represents a rare exception in his activities as a collector. Since 1983 the Burrell Collection has been housed in its own building in Pollok Park, a large estate to the south-west of Glasgow, which was gifted to the city by Anne Maxwell Macdonald, together with Pollok House, the home of her grandfather Sir William Stirling Maxwell. Active in public life (he served twice as Member of Parliament for Perthshire), Stirling Maxwell was also a pioneering historian of Spanish painting, and the paintings in his collection are naturally largely Spanish. Included, however, in the present exhibition are two exceptions to this rule: the powerfully expressive *Lamentation* by Signorelli (cat. no. 3), which he inherited from an uncle; and the anonymous *Vanitas* (cat. no. 24), which the owner considered to be Spanish, but which has been shown by recent research to have almost certainly been painted in Rome.

Apart from the pair of landscapes by Rosa received from the Young family in 1952–53, Glasgow Museums acquired two other important Italian pictures in the second half of the twentieth century. These were Titian's *Head of a Man*, a fragment from the cut-down *Christ and the Adulteress* (cat. no. 9) and wisely purchased by Glasgow when it appeared on the London art market in 1971; and Niccolò di Buonaccorso's *St Lawrence* (cat. no. 1), presented in 1980 by the Glasgow jeweller and major benefactor of Glasgow Museums, Julius Lewis Lyons (1905–1999). Although the Lyons bequest of 1999 comprised the first important collection of Italian Old Master drawings to be received by Glasgow Museums, the *St Lawrence* was the only Lyons gift of an Italian painting. On the other hand, as the only example hitherto of an Italian work of the fourteenth century, it had the additional distinction of further extending the chronological range of the collection to more than half a millennium.

Professor Peter Humfrey
University of St Andrews

Bibliographical note

For a full bibliography relating to the artists and issues discussed in this catalogue, see the complete catalogue of Glasgow's Italian paintings – *Glasgow Museums: The Italian Paintings* by Peter Humfrey, co-published by Glasgow Museums and Unicorn Press, London, 2012, ISBN 978-1-906509-17-0.

I

Trecento and Quattrocento :

TRADITION AND DISCOVERY

Trecento and Quattrocento :

TRADITION AND DISCOVERY

For Giorgio Vasari (1511–1574), the great historian of Italian Renaissance art, an epoch-making rebirth in the visual arts began to take place in about the year 1300. In his opinion, the arts had reached perfection in classical antiquity, but had declined into barbarism in the Middle Ages. Then, at the end of the thirteenth century, in the region of Tuscany in central Italy, a gradual process of revival had begun. For Vasari, this revival, or rebirth, was rooted in a renewed study both of external nature and of surviving examples of antique sculpture, and it developed in three stages (beginnings, improvement, perfection) roughly corresponding respectively to the fourteenth (the *Trecento*), fifteenth (the *Quattrocento*) and sixteenth (the *Cinquecento*) centuries. He would have considered Niccolò di Buonaccorso's *St Lawrence* of c. 1370–75 (cat. no. 1) a diligent enough work for its time, but as regrettably remote from nature in its richly wrought surface and plentiful use of gold-leaf. By comparison, he would have accepted that Francia's *Nativity* of 1490 (cat. no. 2) shows enormous advances, in its sculpturally rounded forms, and in the effects of space generated by geometric perspective and distant landscape. Yet Vasari considered Francia's style to be dry and pedantic compared with that of a leading member of the next generation such as Raphael, and as still lacking the ideal beauty of the third stage of development.

Detail from **Adoration of the Magi**, *c.* 1503–10 (?)

Master of the Glasgow *Adoration*
Oil on panel
586
Bequest of Mrs John Graham Gilbert, 1877

Detail from
St Catherine Crowned, *c.* 1520

Bartolomeo Veneto
Oil on panel
210
Archibald McLellan Collection,
purchased 1856

The prestige of the *Lives* was so great that Vasari's historiographic scheme dominated the critical evaluation of Italian Renaissance artists for the next three centuries or more. As noted in the Introduction, Archibald McLellan formed his collection with the express intention of illustrating 'the revival of art (from) the fifteenth century'. Yet he showed little interest in the fifteenth century itself, and the Francia, together with Botticelli's *Annunciation* (cat. no. 4), probably likewise of the 1490s, were his only Italian pictures dating from before 1500. This growing interest in the earlier period from the later nineteenth century among art lovers is to some extent reflected in subsequent gifts, such as the Raffaellino del Garbo (fig. 12), the Signorelli (cat. no. 3), the two Giovanni Bellinis (cat. no. 5; fig. 13), and eventually the Niccolò di Buonaccorso. Even so, early Italian painting remains numerically rather thinly represented in Glasgow Museums.

Yet although few in number, the early pictures in the exhibition are of particular interest and importance, and they complement one another nicely in their subjects, and in the regional schools they represent. Niccolò di Buonaccorso is a rare master, with only a handful of surviving works, and his *St Lawrence* is a very attractive example of the refined and lyrical tradition of the Sienese Trecento. Florentine painting of the late fifteenth century is well represented by Botticelli's *Annunciation*, while the schools of Venice, Bologna and Umbria are represented respectively by the Bellinis and the Catena (cat. no. 6), the Francia, and by Signorelli's powerfully emotional *Lamentation*. Notable among the works that still clearly belong to fifteenth-century tradition, but which probably date from the early years of the sixteenth, are Bartolomeo Veneto's *St Catherine* (cat. no. 7), and the *Adoration of the Magi* (cat. no. 8). The latter, although still anonymous, represents a significant and rare example of painting in this period in the southern city of Naples.

1 *Niccolò di Buonaccorso* (c. 1348–1388)

St Lawrence, c. 1370–75

St Lawrence, who was martyred in Rome under the emperor Valerian in the year 258, was one of the most popular saints in the later Middle Ages. He is immediately recognizable here by his youthful appearance, his deacon's vestment and tonsure, and his attributes of a martyr's palm and a gridiron, the instrument on which he was roasted alive. The panel now presents a somewhat battered appearance, and in places the gold leaf background has worn thin to reveal the red bole layer below. Similarly, the flesh tones have become transparent, and have acquired an excessively green tinge. But it is not difficult to imagine the original richness of effect. The saint's red vestment is decorated on the collar and chest with an intricate diaper (repetitive diagonals/squares) pattern, and his halo is stamped with a fine network of punchmarks.

Nothing is known of the original placing of the panel, but it almost certainly formed part of a now dismembered polyptych, commissioned for the altar of a church in Siena, or in one of its surrounding villages. Typical of this kind of multipanelled altarpiece would have been an arrangement of the panels in two or more tiers, with a Virgin and Child at the centre, full-length standing saints to either side, half-length saints in the upper tier, and further saints – as was probably the case with the present *St Lawrence* – mounted on pinnacles above. The panels would have been contained within a richly carved and gilded Gothic frame, complementing the pointed arches and gold backgrounds of the panels. When illuminated by candlelight during the celebration of mass, the overall effect of the polyptych would have been one of the utmost material magnificence, but also highly evocative of religious mystery, inspiring the faithful to pray to Lawrence and the other saints depicted.

St Lawrence, c. 1370–75

Tempera and gold on panel,
63 x 31.3 cm; 24.8 x 12.3 inches
3359
Given by Julius Lewis Lyons, 1980

1

Niccolò di Buonaccorso

St Lawrence

Although Niccolò di Buonaccorso was a leading painter in late fourteenth-century Siena, surviving works by him are very rare. Another panel, a *Head of the Virgin* now in the Städel Museum, Frankfurt, has been tentatively identified as a fragment of the same altarpiece. Niccolò's style is characteristic of Sienese painters of his generation in being flatter and more delicate than that practised by painters such as the Lorenzetti brothers in the heroic phase before the Black Death, the catastrophic plague epidemic of 1348.

The present panel is the earliest in Glasgow's collection of Italian paintings, but it was also the last to be acquired, having been gifted to Glasgow Museums by Julius Lewis Lyons in 1980.

2 *Francesco Francia* (c. 1450–1517)

The Nativity of Christ, c. 1490

Francia was the leading painter in the north Italian city of Bologna in the last decade of the fifteenth century and the first of the sixteenth, and was closely associated with the ruling family of the Bentivoglio. He specialized in the production of altarpieces for the churches of the city, most of them representing the Virgin and Child enthroned with saints. The mood of these works is typically placid, their compositional rhythms are gentle and harmonious, and the gestures of the figures are unemphatic.

This panel once occupied the centre of the predella, or painted base, of a now dismembered altarpiece. It shows the newborn Child being worshipped by the kneeling figures of the Virgin Mary and two angels; further off stand Joseph and a praying shepherd, and in the sky on the left is another pair of angels, singing in jubilation from a scroll. A fragment of classical architecture on the right is probably meant to refer to the collapse of the pagan order with the coming of Christ. The painter lays great emphasis on spatial clarity, and shows the background stable in elaborate geometric perspective.

Francia's altarpiece was commissioned in about 1490 by the Bolognese nobleman Bartolomeo Felicini for his chapel in the Church of Santa Maria della Misericordia in Bologna. Although this was stripped of its most important works of art at the beginning of the nineteenth century, the Felicini chapel, situated in the right transept, retains its original early Renaissance architectural character. Still in place is the original gilded wooden frame of Francia's altarpiece, consisting of paired Corinthian pilasters decorated with classical ornament. Although they are now widely dispersed, the five constituent panels of the altarpiece fortunately still survive, and it is possible to provide a visual reconstruction of the ensemble (fig. 20). The main panel, now in the Pinacoteca Nazionale, Bologna, shows the *Virgin and Child Enthroned*, accompanied by the kneeling figure of the donor, and a group of standing saints, including John the

The Nativity of Christ, c. 1490

Oil on panel, 32 x 55 cm; 12.6 x 21.7 inches

146

Archibald McLellan Collection, purchased 1856

Baptist as the dedicatee of the chapel, and Francis. Placed above this, in the apex, was the *Dead Christ with Angels*, also now in the Pinacoteca. Below was the predella, with a *Stigmatization of St Francis* (Private Collection) and a *Baptism of Christ* (now in the Gulbenkian Foundation, Lisbon) placed on either side of the central *Nativity*.

Originally these three scenes in the predella were painted on a single long plank, and were divided by painted colonettes, fragments of which can still be seen at the sides. The landscape background was also continuous across the three panels, and some of the natural and architectural features of the *Nativity* are continued into the neighbouring

2

Francesco Francia

The Nativity of Christ

panels. For example, the other half of the temple represented at the far left in the *Nativity* appears at the far right on the *Stigmatization*. All this proves that contrary to normal expectation – whereby the stories in the predella relate to the saints represented directly above them in the main panel – the *Stigmatization* was placed on the left of the *Nativity*, and the *Baptism* on the right. Another unifying element between the three predella panels is that all three include heavenly apparitions in the sky: the crucifix carried by seraphs, the singing angels, and the Dove of the Holy Spirit.

There is also a vertical thematic link between the *Nativity*, and the two larger panels originally placed above. Prominently placed in the central foreground of Glasgow's work, the Christ Child reappears in his mother's arms, and again as the adult Christ, as a sacrificial victim. This alignment would naturally also have tied the three images of Christ with the altar table below, the place of the celebration of mass. Indeed, the way in which the Child in the *Nativity* is placed on an altar-like rock, with ministering angels in attendance, has a distinctly liturgical appearance.

With the widespread suppression of religious institutions during the Napoleonic period, the altarpiece was removed from the church and sent to the local academy of art, the Accademia Clementina. There it was decided that the three predella panels were of lesser artistic value than the main panel and apex, and in 1818 they were sold to a dealer in Rome. In 1826 the *Baptism* and the *Stigmatization* were recorded on the London art market, and it is likely that the *Nativity* reached Britain at about the same time.

Opposite Fig. 20
Reconstruction of Francia's Felicini altarpiece.

3

Luca Signorelli (c. 1450–1523)

Lamentation over the Dead Christ, c. 1488–90

Born in Cortona in southern Tuscany, by c.1482 Luca Signorelli was a member of the team of artists working in the Sistine Chapel in Rome. During the following two decades, in which he painted his finest works, he successfully developed a personal style that was both powerfully sculptural and expressively dynamic. In this period he painted a series of important altarpieces for towns and cities in Tuscany and Umbria such as Siena, Volterra and Città di Castello. His most complex and ambitious work, the fresco decoration of the Cappella Nova (San Brizio Chapel) in Orvieto Cathedral (1499–1503), shows a number of nudes in a wide range of poses, and was, according to

the art historian Giorgio Vasari, a major inspiration for Michelangelo. In the following two decades, however, with the rise of a younger generation of artists, he was no longer highly regarded in the leading centres of Florence and Rome.

In this painting the dead Christ, resembling a youthful hero of classical antiquity, lies in the lap of the Virgin, who has fainted with grief. The pair are surrounded by mourning women, while the frantically gesticulating Mary Magdalen advances from the right. Beside her stand the male figures of Nicodemus and Joseph of Arimathea. In the left background is Golgotha, with the two thieves still on their crosses, and the buildings on the right presumably refer to the city of Jerusalem. Signorelli has composed the figure group in a frieze-like arrangement, recalling that of an antique sarcophagus, tightly squeezed into the picture field above and below, but also infused with a tense rhythmic energy. Decorative unity across the wide format is created by the repetition of colours in the draperies, and of striped fabrics in clothing at the far left and right.

Lamentation over the Dead Christ,
c. 1488–90

Oil (?) on panel, 30 x 120.2 cm;
11.8 x 47.3 inches

PC.25

Bequest of Dame Anne Maxwell
Macdonald, 1967

3

Luca Signorelli

Lamentation over the Dead Christ

The panel originally formed part of the predella of a monumental altarpiece combining painting and sculpture in the Bichi chapel, formerly in the right transept of the Church of Sant'Agostino in Siena. Other surviving components are a polychrome statue of *St Christopher* by Francesco di Giorgio (Louvre, Paris); two painted fragments showing *Two Nude Youths* and *Man, Woman and Child* (Toledo Museum of Art); two principal panels, showing *Sts Eustochium, Jerome and Mary Magdalen* and *Sts Anthony of Padua, Augustine and Catherine of Alexandria* (Staatliche Museen, Berlin); and the remaining two predella panels, showing *Christ in the House of Simon* (National Gallery of Ireland, Dublin) and the *Martyrdom of St Catherine* (Sterling and Francine Clark Institute, Williamstown, MA).

On the basis of an early eighteenth-century description, it has been possible to reconstruct the appearance of the ensemble (fig. 21). The titular saint of the chapel, Christopher, was represented at the centre in the form of Francesco di Giorgio's statue; behind this Signorelli painted a river landscape with bathers. Flanking the central image were the two groups of three standing and kneeling saints, set under architectural canopies against a continuation of the landscape. The predella, originally consisting of a single long plank, was divided into three by ornamental candelabra; the two at the sides show scenes from the lives of two of the female saints above them, Mary Magdalen and Catherine. In its place at the centre of the predella the *Lamentation* would have reinforced the Christological significance of the statue above (Christopher = Christ-bearer), and the meaning of the eucharistic sacrifice of the mass celebrated directly in front of it.

The dedication of the chapel to Christopher, and the inclusion of Jerome's disciple Eustochia in the left main panel, were clearly the choice of its founder Eustochia Bichi,

Fig. 21 : Professor Max Seidel's 1984 reconstruction of the Bichi altarpiece.

widow of one Cristoforo Bellanti. When she founded it in 1487 her father, the Sienese banker Antonio Bichi, assumed responsibility for funding the decoration, including the altarpiece. It is probable that the altarpiece was commissioned soon after the foundation of the chapel, and was completed by 1490.

The altarpiece was removed from the church some time in the mid eighteenth century, and was dismembered. In the nineteenth century the *Lamentation* belonged to Sir William Stirling Maxwell, who apparently inherited it from his uncle James Stirling of Keir (1766–1831). Since all three of the predella panels are recorded on the London art market in the early years of that century, it is likely that they arrived in Britain from Italy as parts of a single long plank, which was then sawn apart so that they could be sold as three separate pictures.

4 *Sandro Botticelli* (1444/5–1510)

The Annunciation, *c.* 1490–95

In the gospel story of the Annunciation (Luke 1: 26–38), the Angel Gabriel visits Mary in Nazareth to tell her that she has been chosen to give birth to the Son of God. This was one of the most popular subjects in fifteenth-century Florentine painting, in large part because of the close association of ideas between the flowering lily traditionally carried by the Angel Gabriel (a symbol of the Virgin's purity) and the name of Florence and its floral civic emblem. The story, involving a combination of interior and exterior spaces, also gave painters the opportunity to experiment with the recently formulated laws of geometric perspective. Botticelli shows the angel as if running towards the Virgin in her bedchamber, while the golden rays above mark the miraculous passage of the Holy Spirit from God. The Virgin's pose expresses both her awe ('she cast in her mind what manner of salutation this should be') and her humble obedience to God's will ('Behold the handmaid of the Lord; be it unto me according to thy word'). Beyond the courtyard on the left is a garden, certainly meant to signify the *hortus conclusus* (enclosed garden) – a symbol of Mary's chastity based on the Song of Songs (4:12) – even though the garden is not in fact enclosed, but looks on to a lake and hillside. The painted architecture, with its contrasting use of grey stone *(pietra serena)* for the members and mouldings and white stucco for the walls and vaults, is characteristically Florentine, and although somewhat schematized, recalls the work of contemporary architects such as Giuliano da Sangallo and Cronaca.

The Annunciation, *c.* 1490–95
Oil, tempera and gold leaf on walnut panel, 49.5 x 61.9 cm; 19.5 x 24.4 inches
Inscribed on the back 'Botticelli/Dalla Galleria Ri.ani/....dalla Chiesa/San B.rna.../di Firenze'
174
Archibald McLellan Collection, purchased 1856

4

Sandro Botticelli

The Annunciation

The fragmentary inscription on the back ('Botticelli/Dalla Galleria Ri.ani/....dalla Chiesa/San B.rna.../di Firenze') has been convincingly interpreted as identifying the picture's original location as San Barnaba in Florence, a church of Augustinian canons for which Botticelli painted the main altarpiece in about 1485 (now in the Uffizi Gallery, Florence). The *Annunciation* could not, however, have formed part of the altarpiece, and must have been placed elsewhere in the church or its adjoining convent.

Botticelli was one of the leading painters of late fifteenth-century Florence, and by the 1470s he had developed the elegantly linear style for which he is famous. It may be noted that despite the deep space created by the perspective lines of the architecture in the present work, the representation of the figures is rather flat, with a strong emphasis on decorative, flowing outlines. The poses are also rather unstable, with the angel dancing in on tiptoe, and the Virgin leaning forwards to meet him on an answering diagonal. Also characteristic of Botticelli is the way in which the lines of the architecture are sharply incised into the layer of white priming between the panel support and the paint layers. An oddity of the representation of the architecture is that the pier dividing the two spaces is not perpendicular to the ground, but leans slightly to the left, and that its two sides are not parallel to one another. This has been interpreted alternatively as a deliberate expressive device, contributing to the drama and tension of the scene, or as evidence that the execution of the painting was delegated to a workshop assistant, whose imitation of the master's style was not entirely successful.

Given the extraordinary interest in Botticelli shown by British artists and critics in the later nineteenth century, the picture is remarkable for being one of the first by the artist to be imported from Italy to England. When the Rev. John Sanford (1777–1855) bought it in the 1830s from the collection assembled by the Avvocato Rivani in Florence, only

two other Botticellis had reached England. During his five years of residence in Florence (1832–37), Sanford acquired a considerable number of Florentine Quattrocento pictures, including works by (or attributed to) Fra Angelico, Fra Filippo Lippi, and other painters still largely unknown in Britain. But soon after his return to London, Sanford sold a large part of his collection, including the Botticelli, which fetched only £4–12s (about £465/$750 in today's currency). Although it is not clear exactly when it was acquired by McLellan, the entry of the *Annunciation* into Glasgow Museums' collection preceded the first acquisition of a genuine Botticelli by the National Gallery, London, by three years. McLellan may, however, have regarded his picture as no more than a copy, since it is recorded as such in the 1855 catalogue of his collection.

5

Giovanni Bellini (c. 1435/8–1516)

Virgin and Child, c. 1480–85

Giovanni Bellini, the greatest painter of early Renaissance Venice, made a lifelong speciality of creating half-length images of the Virgin and Child. Unlike his grander, full-length representations of the Virgin Enthroned, usually painted for the formal and liturgical setting of a church, such images were certainly intended to be displayed in the home, probably in a bedroom. There they could perhaps serve as a focus for private prayer, or express the owner's hope for divine blessing in their everyday lives.

Here the Christ Child is shown in the very act of blessing, although it is difficult to say why he turns his attention downwards to the left, as if towards an unseen supplicant. Characteristic of Bellini are the seriousness with which he performs the gesture, and the thoughtfully introspective expression on the face of the Virgin. Although the painter invests his holy figures with a convincing humanity, conveying the tenderness of the relationship between a mother and her child, he never forgets that they are also divine. It is as if they are already conscious of Christ's future self-sacrifice on the cross, and of their roles in the redemption of mankind.

Virgin and Child, c. 1480–85

Tempera and oil on panel,
62.3 x 46.2 cm; 24.5 x 18.2 inches

575

Bequest of Mrs John Graham
Gilbert, 1877

Perhaps the marble ledge on which the Child stands is meant to suggest the sarcophagus on which he was to be buried on Good Friday. Certainly it provides a solid base for the imposing pyramidal composition, and helps situate the figures in a clearly defined space, on the other side of a sort of window, with the ledge forming the sill. At this stage of his career, probably in the early 1480s, Bellini was deeply concerned with conveying the effect of round volume. This may be seen in his careful modelling in light and shade, and in his use of devices such as the sharp foreshortening of Christ's right hand and forearm. In these years he also pioneered the use of the oil medium, and exploited it to create more gradual and subtle tonal transitions than were possible with the traditional technique of egg tempera. Unfortunately, the present condition of the painting is not good, and much

5

Giovanni Bellini

Virgin and Child

of the original pictorial effect has been severely compromised. The Virgin's red robe has been overpainted, giving it a blotchy appearance, and the modelling of her blue cloak is difficult to read. The flesh tones have also become thin and transparent. But this last effect at least allows us to appreciate with the naked eye the beauty and sensitivity of the artist's underdrawing, which conveys shading through delicate parallel hatchings.

Note

This painting had, presumably since it was accessioned into Glasgow's collection, been displayed in an elaborate rococo-style gilt frame. The frame was stylistically inappropriate for a religious painting of this type and age, and in 2011 Glasgow Museums commissioned a high-quality reproduction, visually more suitable, frame. The appearance and fabrication of the new frame follow that of surviving examples of Venetian frames from the Renaissance period. Funding for the frame was generously provided by the Friends of Glasgow Museums (FoGM).

6   *Vincenzo Catena* (c. 1470/80–1531)

Virgin and Child with St Mary Magdalen and Another Female Saint, c. 1500–05

The Venetian painter Catena was a close follower of Giovanni Bellini, and in his early career he exploited the market created by his master for half-length representations of the Virgin and Child (cat. no. 5). The central figure group in this work is directly based, in fact, on one by Bellini himself, as seen in a painting now in Frankfurt. Catena also follows Bellini in representing a marble ledge at the base of his composition, which serves both as a spatial device, separating the space of the holy figures from that of the spectator, and as a surface on which the painter can place his (now much damaged) signature. Bellini was also responsible for introducing this type of variant of his own vertical compositions, in which the Virgin and Child are seen alone, by expanding the format horizontally, allowing the inclusion of flanking saints.

The saint on the right is clearly identifiable as Mary Magdalen, holding the jar of ointment with which she bathed Christ's feet. Perhaps her elaborate hair-style is meant to refer to the vanity and worldliness of her early life. The saint on the left is much harder to identify. It has sometimes been supposed that she is Agatha, who was tortured by her pagan persecutors by cutting her breasts off. But her right breast and shoulder are clearly not meant to be shown as naked, but covered by a tight-fitting garment in common with many female saints in Venetian paintings of the period. The clue to her identity is more likely to be provided by her crown of leaves. If these are olive leaves, she may be Olive, an obscure saint, but one whose relics are preserved in the Venetian mainland city of Brescia.

The hard surfaces of the draperies and the enamel-like colours suggest that this is one of the painter's earliest works, probably dating from soon after 1500.

Virgin and Child with St Mary Magdalen and Another Female Saint, *c.* 1500–05

Oil on panel, 71.5 x 87.2 cm; 28.1 x 34.3 inches

Inscribed with a now fragmentary signature on the ledge: VINZENZIVS-CA[T]ENA

199

Archibald McLellan Collection, purchased 1856

7

Bartolomeo Veneto (c. 1480–1531)

St Catherine Crowned, *c.* 1520

The figure is identifiable as St Catherine of Alexandria by her attribute of a spiked wheel. Her crown consisting of flowers of white jasmine, which may be interpreted as a reference to her purity, is also appropriate to her status as a princess and virgin martyr. Yet she lacks a halo, and the suggestiveness of her smile makes the painting resemble not so much the devotional image of a saint as a secular image, of a type known as 'beautiful woman'. This type, which was very popular in Venetian and Lombard painting in the first three decades of the sixteenth century, consisted of representations of young women in a half-length, portrait-like format. They were not, however, meant to be portraits of real people, but were idealized beauties, designed to stir the erotic longings of the male viewer.

Bartolomeo's biography is obscure, but a *Virgin and Child* of 1502 (Private Collection) is clearly based on the work of the Venetian painter Giovanni Bellini (cat. no. 5), while an inscription on the same picture alludes to his probable birth in the Lombard city of Cremona. By 1511, he had left Venice for Milan, where his Venetian style fused with one inspired by Leonardo da Vinci. Indeed, Leonardo's *Virgin of the Rocks* of *c.* 1485 (Louvre, Paris) may be seen as an obvious source for the figure, with her tightly curled ringlets, and the softly rounded oval of her head emerging from a dark background, as well as for the disturbing ambivalence of her expression. But very different from Leonardo's style is the metallic precision of the detail, which has a flattening rather than spatial effect.

St Catherine Crowned, c. 1520
Oil on panel, 35.5 x 28 cm; 14 x 11 inches
210
Archibald McLellan Collection, purchased 1856

8

Master of the Glasgow Adoration (active c. 1490–1520)

Adoration of the Magi, c. 1503–10 (?)

As the three gorgeously attired kings move forward to pay homage to the Christ Child, their retinue is seen in the right background. The artist conforms to a well-established tradition by showing them to be of contrasting ages. The eldest, with a long white beard, has already set his crown on the floor as he kneels before the Virgin and Child and presents his gift of gold. The second king is in the act of doffing his crown; the third still gazes up at the star that has guided them to Bethlehem. Also traditional is the idea that the stable where Christ was born was constructed in the ruins of a pagan temple. This refers to the belief that on the night of the Nativity the Basilica of Maxentius in the Roman Forum suddenly crumbled, thereby demonstrating that the world of pagan antiquity was about to make way for the new era of Christianity. Clearly visible inside the ruined temple is a sculptured triptych, incorporating what are meant to be images of pagan gods.

The appearance of the panel has improved dramatically since its cleaning in 2011–12 in preparation for this exhibition. Previously it was covered with a thick layer of darkened varnish that obscured the brilliance of the colour and of the extensive gilding. The gilding was used for the brocade of the draperies, and also for the raised ornamentation made of gesso, known as *pastiglia*, used for the crowns, gifts, necklaces and other decorative details.

The identity of the artist remains mysterious, and since this is his most important known work, he has been dubbed the 'Master of the Glasgow *Adoration*'. It has been suggested that he may originally have been from Spain, but it is equally likely that he was a native Neapolitan. In any case, from his style it has been inferred that he was active at the Spanish vice-regal court in Naples, probably at the beginning of the sixteenth century. Presumably the panel formed part of a polyptych, and to judge from

Adoration of the Magi,
c. 1503–10 (?)

Oil on panel, 180.4 x 94.3 cm;
71 x 37.1 inches

586

Bequest of Mrs John Graham
Gilbert, 1877

the perspective lines, which converge to a point well right of centre, it was matched by another narrative scene to the right. Two smaller panels (171 x 78 cm; 67.3 x 30.7 inches each), representing *St Louis of Toulouse* and *St Augustine* (both Alte Pinakothek, Munich), have been proposed as having once belonged to the same complex.

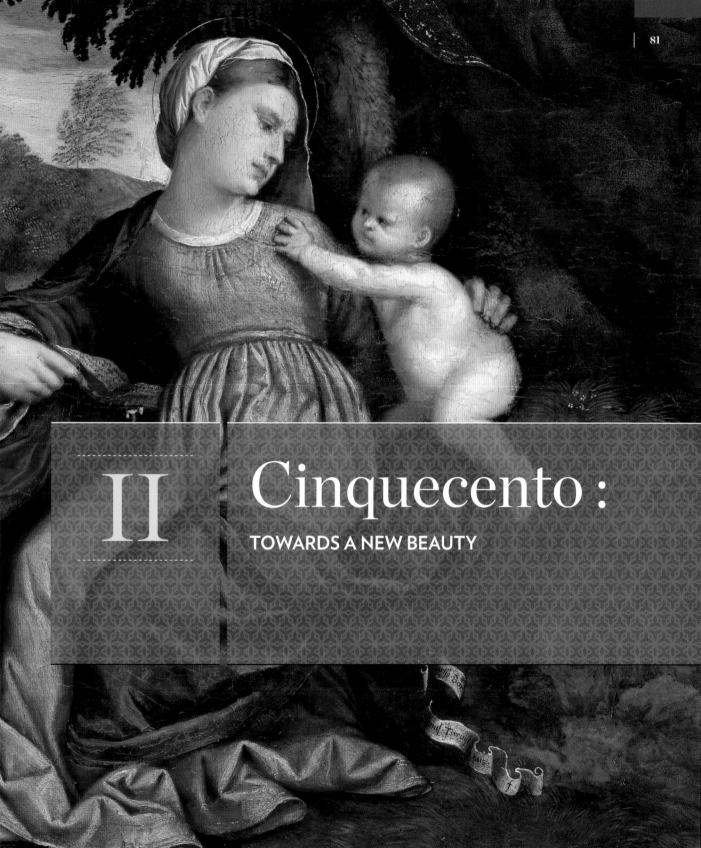

II Cinquecento :

TOWARDS A NEW BEAUTY

Cinquecento :

TOWARDS A NEW BEAUTY

For Vasari, the modern revival of the visual arts reached a pinnacle in the first decades of the sixteenth century (the Cinquecento), under the leadership of the three great central Italians Leonardo da Vinci, Michelangelo and Raphael. Vasari also had high admiration, albeit with some reservations, for their north Italian contemporaries Giorgione, Titian and Correggio. For the author, all these masters possessed a command of the representation of nature that went far beyond that of previous generations, while also attaining a grace and fluency that surpassed even the art of classical antiquity. Even lesser figures of the same generation, such as the Venetian Palma Vecchio (fig. 17), or the Ferrarese Garofalo, reached a higher level of excellence than would have been accessible to their fifteenth-century predecessors. Artists of the succeeding generation, such as Parmigianino and Girolamo da Carpi (cat. no. 12) – members of Vasari's own generation – similarly benefited from the example of the great leaders, and could achieve new effects of beauty by introducing a greater refinement, virtuosity and complexity.

Detail from **Virgin and Child in a Landscape with the Child Baptist and St Catherine of Alexandria,** *c.* 1545
Girolamo da Carpi
Oil on panel
1587
Bequeathed by Sir Claude Phillips, 1924

Detail from **Virgin and Child with Saints John the Baptist, Mary Magdalen and George (?)**, *c.* 1524
Paris Bordon
Oil on panel
191
Archibald McLellan Collection, purchased 1856

There remains, however, an uneasy sense in Vasari, who was much attached to the biological metaphor of growth, flowering and decay, that the art of his own generation might represent a decline from an earlier pinnacle of perfection. Indeed, critics and historians from the seventeenth century onwards, while almost unanimously following Vasari in the high esteem that he accorded to the great generation of Michelangelo and Raphael, have until recently tended to regard Italian painting of the later sixteenth century as deplorably decadent.

A natural consequence of the universal admiration in which the short-lived Raphael and Correggio were held was that the demand for their work among collectors far exceeded the available supply, and only moderately wealthy latecomers such as McLellan had to be content with copies. Even the work of lesser central Italians could be hard to come by, since many of them, like Michelangelo himself, were more active as painters of murals than of moveable easel pictures. For this reason, works by north Italians and Venetians, who customarily worked on canvas, were much more abundant. This was true even of Titian, who was highly productive, thanks to a long career and a team of studio assistants. As for Giorgione, although by the twentieth century he had become one of the rarest of Old Masters, the uncertainty surrounding his output meant that in earlier periods an extraordinarily large number of pictures were optimistically associated with his name.

Against this background, it is not surprising that Glasgow owns more Italian pictures from the sixteenth than from any other century. Slightly less expected is the fact that the overwhelming majority are religious in content, with almost no mythological subjects,

Detail from **St James Major and St Catherine of Alexandria**, *c.* 1565
Orazio Sammacchini
Oil on white metal
164
Archibald McLellan Collection, purchased 1856

or even portraits. By far the most important work from the so-called High Renaissance period is the *Christ and the Adulteress* (cat. no. 9), one of the most famous objects in Glasgow's collection. Attributed to Titian's follower Bonifacio de' Pitati when in the McLellan collection, and then for more than a century to Giorgione, this impressive picture is still not unanimously accepted as by Titian. This is largely because as an early work it is not yet absolutely typical of him.

The collection is strong on other Venetian painters of the Cinquecento as well, including Palma Vecchio, Paris Bordon (cat. nos. 10, 11), Tintoretto, and several lesser figures, all of whom may be regarded as followers of Titian in their taste for warm, glowing colour and sensuous pictorial effects. But almost as strongly represented in the collection are painters from a number of other north Italian centres of the early to mid sixteenth century, including the Ferrarese Garofalo and Girolamo da Carpi, the Bolognese Orazio Sammacchini (cat. no. 13), the Brescian Lattanzio Gambara, and the Cremonese Camillo Boccaccino. While several of these might in previous decades have been labelled pejoratively as Mannerists, and as representative of a decadent phase in Italian painting, today they may be appreciated as still impressively vital in their sense of ornamental elegance. Further, it is to the credit of Glasgow Museums that most of them are otherwise poorly represented in British collections, including the National Gallery, London. All this is even more true of a major work painted in Rome at the very end of the century: the Cavaliere d'Arpino's exquisite *Archangel Michael and the Rebel Angels* of *c.* 1592–93 (cat. no. 15).

9 *Titian (Tiziano Vecellio)* (c. 1488/90–1576)

Christ and the Adulteress. c. 1508–10 and Head of a Man, c. 1508–10

Probably the most famous Italian painting in Glasgow's collections, the *Christ and the Adulteress* was originally some 12 to 20 inches wider than it is now, and included a full-length standing figure of a man at the far right of the composition. This figure survives as a fragment, the *Head of a Man*, which was purchased by Glasgow Museums in 1971, more than a century after the bequest of the main canvas. A good idea of the original composition is provided by a not quite exact copy in Bergamo (fig. 22), from which it can be seen that the triangular shape overlapping the woman's dress at the lower right edge of the main canvas corresponds to the standing man's left knee. Why the canvas was cut down is unknown. But the paint surface shows signs of damage in the right foreground, and it may be that the lower part of the male figure was ruined, and that a dealer decided that the work would be more marketable as two separate paintings.

The subject has sometimes been identified as Daniel and Susanna, an episode described in an apocryphal addition to the Old Testament Book of Daniel. This tells of how the virtuous Susanna was falsely accused of adultery by two corrupt elders, but was saved from death by Daniel, who established her accusers' guilt. But the older identification of the subject as Christ and the Adulteress, a rather popular subject in Venetian painting of the early sixteenth century, remains more convincing. The story is recounted in John 8: 2–11. Seeking to trap Jesus

Christ and the Adulteress, c. 1508–10

Oil on canvas, 139.2 x 181.7 cm; 54.8 x 71.5 inches

181

Archibald McLellan Collection, purchased 1856

9

Titian (Tiziano Vecellio)

Christ and the Adulteress and Head of a Man

Fig. 22 : Copy after Titian, *Christ and the Adulteress*, Accademia Carrara, Bergamo

into refusing to support Mosaic law, the Pharisees brought before him a woman who had been discovered in the act of adultery, and demanded that she be stoned to death. Besides showing compassion towards the woman, Jesus disarmed her accusers by saying 'He that is without sin among you, let him first cast a stone at her'. It is true that in a departure from the gospel account, the scene in this painting is set in the open air, not in the temple, and of the various bystanders, only the robed figure on the far left has the appearance of a Pharisee. But in keeping with the gospel story is Christ's leaning pose, as if he has just risen from stooping to write on the ground. The medallion of a Roman emperor, set into the wall above him, serves to locate the event in the period of the New Testament.

9

Titian (Tiziano Vecellio)

Head of a Man

Head of a Man, c. 1508-10

Oil on canvas, 53.8 x 43.6 cm;
21.2 x 17.2 inches

3283

Purchased by Glasgow Museums,
1971

Even more controversial than the identification of the subject has been the identification of the artist. For more than a century after Archibald McLellan bequeathed his collection to his native city the painting was known as the 'Glasgow Giorgione'. Although Giorgione (c. 1477–1510) has always been regarded, from within a few decades of his early death, as one of the great pioneers of Venetian painting of the sixteenth century, his work remains very difficult to define. During the first half of the twentieth century a majority of scholars accepted that the *Christ and the Adulteress* corresponded to the style practised by Giorgione at the end of his short life. Since the 1960s, however, this view has steadily given way to an alternative attribution to Giorgione's younger Venetian contemporary, Titian. A problem with this attribution is that the painting is not entirely typical of Titian, whose work during his long life is very well documented indeed. But it is reasonable, nevertheless, to interpret the *Christ and the Adulteress* as a very early work, painted when he was only about 20, but when he was already highly ambitious. The painting shows a number of faults: it is not quite clear, for example, how the various figures are positioned in space, and some of their anatomies are articulated somewhat awkwardly. But the painting is executed with a magnificent boldness. The figures are highly energetic in their movement, and the palette shows an extraordinary warmth and richness. The painter has clearly also taken delight in employing a wide range of pigments, and in portraying an equally wide range of contrasting surface textures.

Despite the exceptional art-historical importance of this painting, nothing is known of its early history, or of where it was originally placed. But one attractive possibility is that it was painted for the large, well-lit reception room on the main floor of a Venetian palace.

10 *Paris Bordon* (1500–1571)

Virgin and Child with Saints Jerome and Anthony Abbot and a Donor, *c.* 1522

As he indicates in his signature (see caption below), Paris Bordon was born in Treviso, on the Venetian mainland. But he came to Venice as a child and received his artistic education under Titian, and by the 1520s was producing his own versions of the whole range of genres of painting practised by his master. Later in his career he enjoyed a certain international success, and paid extended visits to Milan and the French court at Fontainebleau in 1538.

Datable to about 1522, this is one of the earliest of Bordon's many contributions to the theme of the Virgin and Child informally seated with a group of saints in an idyllic pastoral landscape. Popularized by Titian and Palma Vecchio (fig. 17), this theme enjoyed great success in Venice in the second and third decades of the sixteenth century. Another, probably slightly earlier example by Bordon, in which the figure of Anthony Abbot is almost identical, is in a private collection (fig. 23); yet another, probably slightly later, is in this exhibition (cat. no. 11). In the present work, a kneeling donor is being encouraged by his patron saint, Anthony Abbott, to approach the Virgin and Child, while St Jerome, who spent many years as a penitent in the wilderness, draws the donor's attention to his attribute of a crucifix on the ground. Although the subject is timeless, the compositional type carries natural reminiscences of stories from Christ's infancy such as the Adoration of the Magi, and especially the Rest on the Flight into Egypt, which likewise calls for a landscape

Virgin and Child with Saints Jerome and Anthony Abbot and a Donor, *c.* 1522

Oil on poplar panel, 61 x 82.9 cm; 24 x 32.6 inches
Inscribed on the scroll: Pariss. Bordonus. Taruisi/nus. f
570
Bequest of Mrs John Graham Gilbert, 1877

10

Paris Bordon

Virgin and Child with Saints Jerome and Anthony Abbot and a Donor

setting. The Rest on the Flight was, in fact, another of Bordon's favourite subjects, and an association with the theme may also account for the motif of the curtain on the right, slung over a rustic pole as if to create a makeshift tent. But other details, such as the reclining shepherds with their sheep in the left background, and the rustic building in the centre, are indebted more generally to the type of pastoral landscape evolved by Titian after about 1510 for subjects both sacred and secular.

Bordon's pictorial handling differs from that of his master in combining passages of breadth and freedom with a graphic precision that recalls rather the work of Giorgione, as in the delicate brushstrokes that describe Jerome's beard, and the rhythmical stippling of the foliage. The figures are also slighter of build than Titian's, and less infused with physical energy. This evidence of Bordon deliberately imitating the style of Giorgione, who had died in 1510, conforms with the later report by Vasari that the young Bordon was dissatisfied with Titian as a teacher, and 'grieved much that Giorgione was then dead, for that master's style pleased him exceedingly, and he thought much more of Giorgione's reputation of being a willing and careful teacher of what he knew. Not being able to do better, Paris resolved to adopt Giorgione's style'.

The earliest record of the picture dates from the mid seventeenth century, when the kneeling donor was identified as one Dr Genova, a physician who also came from Treviso, and who presumably for this reason commissioned the picture from his young compatriot. Genova's first name is not known, and Anthony Abbot may have been included as his name saint; it is equally likely that Genova chose him because of his medical associations as a protector against disease and the plague. Surprisingly for a physician, but presumably indicating that he had chivalric pretensions besides considerable wealth, the donor's luxurious costume includes a pair of spurs.

Fig. 23
Paris Bordon,
*Virgin and Child with St Anthony
Abbot and a Donor*,
Private Collection

From Venice the picture passed to the collection of Cardinal Giovan Carlo de' Medici
(1611–63), younger brother of Ferdinando II, Grand Duke of Tuscany, and subsequently
to the Chigi Collection in Rome. There it was acquired in 1800 by the Scottish dealer
James Irvine for Alexander 'Picture' Gordon of Drum (1765–1849), at whose sale in
1837 in Edinburgh, Scotland, it was bought by John Graham Gilbert.

In the posthumous inventory of Giovan Carlo de' Medici of 1663 the two figures on
the left are described as 'two friars', and it seems that it was the cardinal who decided
that Dr Genova, with his portrait-like features and rich costume, should be overpainted
to become an anonymous cleric. When this overpaint was removed in a restoration of
1981–85, a left foot was revealed immediately in front of the donor. As in the picture in
a private collection (fig. 23), this was clearly intended to belong to Anthony Abbot. But
shifted for some reason to the left, it renders his pose inexplicable.

11 *Paris Bordon* (1500–1571)

Virgin and Child with Saints John the Baptist, Mary Magdalen and George (?), c. 1524

Like his somewhat earlier *Virgin and Child with Saints Jerome and Anthony Abbot and a Donor* (cat. no. 10), this represents an early example of one of Paris Bordon's favourite and most characteristic subjects, with the saints grouped informally against a serene pastoral landscape. The Baptist and the Magdalen are clearly identifiable by their respective attributes of a lamb and reed cross, and of an ointment jar, but the armoured saint does not carry the banner that would definitely identify him either as St George, the object of a lively cult in Venice, or as St Liberale, patron saint of Bordon's native city of Treviso. Understated allusions to Christ's future Passion are provided by the sacrificial lamb, to which the Baptist draws the spectator's attention, and by the goldfinch that the Child clutches in his left hand.

Characteristic of Venetian painting of the period are the warm colour range, the glowing intensity of the reds and the blues, and the poetically atmospheric landscape. Equally characteristic are the numerous alterations to the placing of the figures during the pictorial execution, as revealed by X-radiography. The composition is rather grander than that of *Virgin and Child with Saints Jerome and Anthony Abbot and a Donor*, with the Virgin elevated on a rustic throne, and the view of the landscape blocked on the right by stately classicizing architecture. The compositional rhythms are also rather more complex, and the dynamic, spatially conceived pose of the Virgin reflects the painter's knowledge of her counterpart in a major contemporary work by Titian, the Ca' Pesaro altarpiece of c. 1519–26 (Church of the Frari, Venice). But while probably slightly later than Bordon's other Glasgow picture, datable to c. 1522, the present work still retains much in common with works by Titian in the previous decade, and a date of c. 1524 seems likely.

Virgin and Child with Saints John the Baptist, Mary Magdalen and George (?), c. 1524

Oil on panel, 86 x 117.6 cm; 33.9 x 46.3 inches

191

Archibald McLellan Collection, purchased 1856

Presumably the painting corresponds to 'A very beautiful and richly coloured Picture of the Virgin & Child with St George, St Catherine, St Agnes and others in a landscape by Titian or Giorgione' bought by Archibald McLellan from the dealer John Smith in London in November 1841 for £250 (about £25,300/$40,700 today), despite the inaccuracy of the description and the attribution.

12 | *Girolamo da Carpi* (c. 1501–1556)

Virgin and Child in a Landscape with the Child Baptist and St Catherine of Alexandria, *c.* 1545

This scene conflates two quite separate stories – the Mystic Marriage of St Catherine with the Christ Child; and the meeting of the Holy Family with the Child Baptist on their way back from Egypt to Nazareth. This latter episode formed part of a legend popularized by late medieval devotional writers such as the Franciscan Pseudo-Bonaventure and the Dominican Domenico Cavalca. In keeping with customary iconography, the painter shows the two holy children tenderly embracing, while Joseph in the middleground occupies himself with watering the ox and the ass. In the storm clouds at the upper right, musician angels celebrate the meeting by performing a concert.

Girolamo da Carpi was born and trained in Ferrara, the seat of a flourishing Renaissance court ruled by the Este dynasty. After a brief early period of activity in Bologna, da Carpi returned to his native city, where he served two successive dukes, Alfonso I and his son Ercole II. When in Bologna he came into contact with the highly refined art of Parmigianino (1503–1540), and adopted his elegantly elongated figure style, combining it with that of Ferrarese painters such as Dosso Dossi and da Carpi's former master Garofalo. This combination of elements is clearly visible in this work, which probably dates from *c.* 1545, around the middle of the painter's career. Similar angelic concerts frequently occur in the work of his former master Garofalo, while the mysteriously twilit landscape, with its stormclouds and poetic sunset sky, is indebted to Dosso. By contrast, the figures are clearly inspired by Parmigianino, as is particularly evident in the princessly St Catherine, with her long, slender proportions, and the shot-silk effects in her draperies.

Virgin and Child in a Landscape with the Child Baptist and St Catherine of Alexandria, c. 1545

Oil on panel, 61.5 x 82.1 cm; 24.2 x 32.3 inches
1587
Bequeathed by Sir Claude Phillips, 1924

13 | *Orazio Sammacchini* (c. 1532–1577)

St James Major and St Catherine of Alexandria, *c.* 1565

Sammacchini is representative of the Mannerism current in mid to late sixteenth-century Bologna. This work is characteristic of him in the blend of the heroic styles of Raphael and Michelangelo, combined with a somewhat artificial elegance in the poses, and a self-conscious prettiness of colour. Previously the picture was attributed to the Roman painter Taddeo Zuccari (1529–66), and indeed, the two painters' works are often very close in style, especially as the result of working together on the decoration of the Scala Regia in the Vatican (1563–65). This collaboration provides a likely date of *c.* 1565 for the present work. The two saints, each of whom receives a martyr's crown from a flying angel, are clearly identifiable by their attributes. James carries a pilgrim's staff and hat, a reference to one of the most important pilgrimage destinations of the Middle Ages, his shrine at Santiago de Compostella, in north-west Spain. At Catherine's feet are the instruments of her martyrdom, a shattered wheel and a sword.

It has recently been discovered that Archibald McLellan bought the picture for £12 from the Bond Street dealer John Smith in June 1843. In Smith's records it is described as 'St James standing in a landscape, an angel boy hovers above holding a wreath of glory over the head of each Saint, by Zucchero from Strawberry Hill collection'. In the catalogue of the sale of this collection dating from a year earlier, it appears as 'St. James and St. Catherine as Pilgrims, crowned by an Angel, very highly finished, rich in colour and perfect in effect, by Zucchero'. The collection had been formed by one of the greatest English connoisseurs of the eighteenth century, the writer Horace Walpole (1717–97), and was housed in his celebrated neo-Gothic villa of Strawberry Hill at Twickenham. Glasgow's painting is, in fact, clearly visible in a watercolour of *The Tribune at Strawberry Hill* by John Carter (Lewis Walpole Library, Yale University), exhibited at the Royal Academy in 1789. It is not clear why Walpole should have regarded an Italian picture of the mid sixteenth century as appropriate for his villa. Perhaps he regarded

St James Major and St Catherine of Alexandria, *c.* 1565

Oil on white metal, 22.8 x 16.8 cm; 9 x 6.6 inches

164

Archibald McLellan Collection, purchased 1856

Zuccari, whose brother Federigo visited London and executed a portrait drawing of Queen Elizabeth, as a sort of honorary Englishman, like Holbein or Van Dyck. In any case, with its small scale and meticulous execution on metal, this would have found a natural place among the portrait miniatures in his cabinet of curiosities.

14 Florentine, later 16th century

St John the Baptist in the Wilderness, c. 1570–75

Clad only in a fur loincloth, the youthful Baptist is shown as a hermit in the desert, filling a cup with water from a stream. His reed cross is entwined with ivy and a ribbon inscribed with his usual motto, 'Ecce Agnus Dei' (Behold the Lamb of God). The broken stump on the right may refer to his words 'Every tree which bringeth not forth good fruit is hewn down' (Matthew 3:10), prophesying the destruction of the old order with the coming of Christ.

The painting is a characteristic example of the Mannerist style current in Florence in the mid to late sixteenth century. For the past 40 years it has carried an official attribution to Alessandro Allori (1535–1607), and indeed, the pale, smooth-limbed figure of the Baptist, silhouetted against a dark background, is clearly indebted to the example of the leading Florentine painter of the mid sixteenth century, Bronzino, who was Allori's master. But Allori's compositions tend to be even more calculatedly planar, and his figures' limbs typically have a sculptural polish, whereas the figure's pose in this picture is more actively engaged with three-dimensional space, and the flesh is somewhat softer and more naturalistic. Accordingly, not all scholars have accepted the attribution to him, and a number of alternative names have been proposed, including those of Santi di Tito (1536–1603), Giovanni Battista Naldini (1537–1591), and Girolamo Macchietti (1535–1592), all of whom collaborated with Allori on the decoration of the Studiolo of the Grand Duke Francesco I in the Palazzo Vecchio, Florence, between 1570 and 1572. Despite the obvious points of contact with all three of these, however, they do not seem sufficiently close to clinch the attribution to any of them, and for the time being it is probably prudent to leave the picture without a certain author, but with a dating close to the execution of the Studiolo.

St John the Baptist in the Wilderness, c. 1570–75

Oil on panel, 53.4 x 40.9 cm; 21 x 16.1 inches

1588

Bequeathed by Sir Claude Phillips, 1924

15

Cavaliere d'Arpino (Giuseppe Cesari) (c. 1568–1640)

Archangel Michael and the Rebel Angels, c. 1592–93

In a well-established iconography based on the Book of Revelation (12:7–9) (and elaborated in the *Golden Legend*, CXLV, a medieval encyclopaedia of saint lore compiled by Jacobus de Voragine), the warrior Archangel Michael is seen triumphing over Satan (in the form of a dragon) and his rebel angels, and casting them out of heaven.

The painter – always known by his papal title of the Cavaliere d'Arpino – painted at least six versions of this composition, all datable to the 1590s. In the past it was assumed that the five smaller versions painted on copper were painted as reduced variants of the only one to be painted on canvas (Burton Constable Hall, Yorkshire; 213 x 317 cm/83.9 x 124.8 inches). But it has been pointed out that the present version shows a number of alterations during the course of execution, which were then repeated in the other versions, making it most likely to be the original. Several of these alterations are visible to the naked eye: in the contours of the figure of Michael; in the position of his sword, which was originally lower; and in the left hand of the nude immediately below the Archangel, which was originally outstretched, but which now clutches the genitals of the nude at the centre. Consistent with the conclusion that the Glasgow picture was the first in the series is the exceptionally high quality of its execution, with its dazzling palette in the costume of Michael, and the miniature-like refinement of the details.

Archangel Michael and the Rebel Angels, c. 1592–93
Oil on tin leaf (?)-coated copper, 57.8 x 41.8 cm; 22.8 x 16.5 inches
153
Archibald McLellan Collection, purchased 1856

15

Cavaliere d'Arpino (Giuseppe Cesari)

Archangel Michael and the Rebel Angels

Typical of the Mannerist style current in Rome and elsewhere in central Italy from the mid to late sixteenth century is the artificially ornamental character of the composition, and the combination of figures borrowed from a variety of sources. It has been pointed out, for example, that the nude falling backwards on the upper left derives from a fresco of *c.* 1530 by the Florentine painter Perino del Vaga (1501–47) in the Palazzo Doria, Genoa, which the Cavaliere could have known from an engraving, while the figure at the bottom right is derived from one of the figures in the frescoes in the papal fortress of Castel Sant'Angelo, Rome (*c.* 1547–49) by the Bolognese painter Pellegrino Tibaldi (1527–96). More generally, the composition, with its avenging deity at the apex and its welter of tumbling male nudes, is inspired by Michelangelo's *Last Judgement* of 1536–41 in the Sistine Chapel, Rome. But the painter has invested his painting with a vitality of pose and brilliance of colour that breathe new life into a style that by this date was beginning to seem old-fashioned.

III Seicento :

RHETORIC AND REALISM

Seicento :

RHETORIC AND REALISM

If the later sixteenth century was dismissed by subsequent generations as a period of decline, the first half of the seventeenth (Seicento) was already admired in its own day as a period of energetic revival of the greatest achievements of the Renaissance. A particularly influential spokesman for this point of view was the antiquarian Giovanni Pietro Bellori, whose 1672 *Lives of the Modern Painters, Sculptors and Architects* heaped praise on Annibale Carracci in particular, for having returned to the true spirit of Raphael and of antique sculpture, and for having likewise achieved a perfect balance between nature and ideal beauty. Bellori had similar admiration for Carracci's Bolognese followers, including Domenichino (cat. no. 16), Guido Reni and Guercino, but rather less for Annibale's contemporary Caravaggio (1571–1610) and his own followers, whom Bellori saw as overdependent on raw nature, and hence as coarse and ugly. The writer was a leading member of the Accademia di San Luca in Rome, and views very similar to his were later to be expressed by the Royal Academy of Painting and Sculpture in Paris, and in the *Discourses* (1769–90) of Sir Joshua Reynolds, first President of the Royal Academy of Arts in London. By the mid nineteenth century, however, and especially because of the hostility of the leading critic John Ruskin, the tide of taste was beginning to turn against the Italian Seicento, and the rise of interest in the fourteenth- and fifteenth-century 'Primitives' took place at the expense of the previously greatly admired Bolognese. Only in the later twentieth century was their reputation largely restored, while that of Caravaggio has soared to unprecedented heights.

Detail from **Death of Cleopatra,**
c. 1645–50

Francesco del Cairo
Oil on canvas
134
Archibald McLellan Collection,
purchased 1856

The late nineteenth-century changes in the critical fortunes of Italian painters of the seventeenth century meant that after 1877 Glasgow Museums received almost no gifts in this area. McLellan, by contrast, who was a generation older than Ruskin, still accepted the received academic canon, and sought to acquire examples of the work of all the major Bolognese painters, as well as some by their Caravaggesque rivals. As with works by Raphael and Correggio, he was probably resigned to the likelihood that he would not be able to acquire an original Reni, and so bought copies. His *Landscape with St Jerome*, on the other hand, is an early masterpiece by Domenichino (cat. no. 16), and the same may be said of the *Adoration of the Magi* by another painter later to be decried by Ruskin, Carlo Dolci (cat. no. 21). As well as acquiring a copy after one of Caravaggio's most famous Roman paintings, McLellan also bought the powerfully Caravaggesque *Virgin and Child with St Anne* by Antiveduto Gramatica (cat. no. 17). This painting makes a fascinating comparison with one similar in subject and composition, but very different in style, Sassoferrato's *Virgin and Child with St Elizabeth and the Child Baptist* (cat. no. 18), from the Graham Gilbert collection.

Detail from
Virgin and Child with St Anne,
c. 1614–17

Antiveduto Gramatica
Oil on canvas
141
Archibald McLellan Collection,
purchased 1856

The great majority of Glasgow's seventeenth-century pictures are religious in subject, with dominant figures. Rather exceptional in the former respect is Francesco del Cairo's highly voluptuous *Death of Cleopatra* (cat. no. 23), which, in the opulence of its forms and in the sensuousness of its pictorial handling, may be regarded as the most completely 'Baroque' work in the exhibition. Also exceptional, but in a very different way, is Domenichino's *St Jerome*, with its tiny figure in a vast, serene and luminous landscape. In dramatic contrast with this early example of the ideal classical landscape are the two wildly romantic scenes from the life of St John the Baptist by Salvator Rosa (cat. nos. 19, 20), with their jagged rocks, tormented trees, and stormy clouds. Although acquired by James Young in 1877, at a time when a taste for Rosa was no longer fashionable, they may now be recognized not only as two of the painter's finest works, but as two of the finest seventeenth-century landscapes in any collection in Britain.

16 *Domenichino* (1581–1641)

Landscape with St Jerome, c. 1610

According to the *Golden Legend* (see p. 106), St Jerome spent four years as a penitent in the 'vast solitude of the desert, burnt with the heat of the sun'. In keeping with a tradition that had developed in Italy from the mid fifteenth century, Domenichino shows the saint using his time as a hermit to translate the Bible into Latin. On the rock that acts as his writing desk are a copy of the scriptures, an inkwell, and a skull serving as a reminder of human mortality. Beside him are his tame lioness, his attribute of a cardinal's hat, and a cross made of sticks.

Likewise in keeping with Renaissance tradition, Domenichino uses the 'desert' setting to explore his interest in landscape painting. The type of landscape represented here, however, is by no means harsh and arid, but is, on the contrary, serene, verdant, and luminous. Receding through a carefully structured sequence of steps from foreground to distant background, it is clearly inspired by the example of Domenichino's teacher and fellow Bolognese Annibale Carracci (1560–1609), and was in turn to form an essential model for younger exponents of the ideal landscape, such as the French painters Claude and Poussin. Domenichino would have consciously intended his idealized vision of the natural world to serve as a commentary on heroic human activity.

Although born and trained in Bologna, Domenichino became one of the leading painters of early seventeeth-century Rome, where his principal commissions consisted of large-scale altarpieces. But in his early career he painted a number of small-scale landscapes, similar to the present work, presumably for aristocratic connoisseurs. Although the original owner of the *St Jerome* is unknown, by 1727 it belonged to one of the most important collectors of the eighteenth century, the 2nd Duke of Orléans, Prince Regent of France. After the French Revolution it was brought to London with the rest of the Orléans collection, and was acquired by Archibald McLellan some time after 1831.

Landscape with St Jerome, *c.* 1610

Oil on panel, 44 x 59.6 cm; 17.3 x 23.5 inches
139
Archibald McLellan Collection, purchased 1856

17   *Antiveduto Gramatica* (c. 1570/1–1626)

Virgin and Child with St Anne, c. 1614–17

The Christ Child, seated on a couch or cradle, reaches out for a pair of cherries offered to him by his grandmother, St Anne, while Mary gazes on. As is usual in representations of the Virgin and Child and the Holy Family, the presence of the fruit almost certainly alludes to the Garden of Eden, and hence to mankind's redemption from Original Sin by Christ and his mother. At least as important to seventeenth-century viewers, however, would have been the domestic intimacy of the scene, aimed at heightening feelings of tender devotion towards the holy figures.

According to Giovanni Baglione, his first biographer, Gramatica was given his unusual baptismal name (meaning 'foreseen') because his father had predicted that he would be born while his parents were journeying from Siena to Rome. From 1591 he was established as a master in the city, and in the following year the young Caravaggio spent a few months in his studio. During this period Gramatica still practised a more old-fashioned style, but after about 1605 he increasingly drew inspiration from the revolutionary art of his former pupil. This is clearly evident here in the unidealized realism of the figures, in the way in which they are brought close to the viewer, and especially in the dramatic contrast of spotlit forms against a deeply shadowed background. Following Caravaggio's sensational career and early death in 1610, Gramatica inherited some of his most eminent patrons, and to some extent his adoption of the style that the younger man had made fashionable may be seen as an opportunistic way of advancing his own career.

Virgin and Child with St Anne, *c.* 1614–17

Oil on canvas, 98.6 x 134.5 cm; 38.8 x 53 inches

141

Archibald McLellan Collection, purchased 1856

18   *Sassoferrato (Giovanni Battista Salvi)* (1609–1685)

Virgin and Child with St Elizabeth and the Child Baptist, 1640s (?)

Called after his birthplace in the Marches, Sassoferrato settled in Rome in about 1640. Rejecting the prevailing baroque style practised by Pietro da Cortona, Sassoferrato favoured one based on a simplified, archaizing classicism that owed much to the early Raphael – several of whose works he copied – and even to fifteenth-century painters such as Perugino. Although active as a painter both of altarpieces and portraits, Sassoferrato's most characteristic works consist of Madonnas and other devotional pictures, evidently painted to meet the needs of domestic piety. As well as drawing extensively on iconic models by venerated earlier masters, the painter made replicas of his own most successful works, retaining the high quality and smooth, meticulous finish of the originals.

While the figure types in this work are typical of the painter, the composition exactly follows that of a print (etching and engraving) by Annibale Carracci dated 1606. Sassoferrato often used prints by or after Carracci and his school for his paintings, but in this case he would also have been attracted to the sculptural and severely tectonic composition, recalling the Holy Family groups of Raphael and other early sixteenth-century painters, with the Christ Child placed at the centre of a saltire cross. Because of the unusual consistency of his style, Sassoferrato's paintings are difficult to date, but it is most likely that this work is from the 1640s, in the period following his arrival in Rome.

Virgin and Child with St Elizabeth and the Child Baptist, 1640s (?)

Oil on canvas, 73.6 x 97.8 cm; 29 x 38.5 inches

584

Mrs John Graham Gilbert Bequest, 1877

19 *Salvator Rosa* (1615–1673)

St John the Baptist Revealing Christ to the Disciples, 1656–57

Despite his lifelong ambition to be a figure painter, Rosa's fame has always rested on his landscapes, which, in contrast to those of the ideal, arcadian tradition represented by Domenichino (see cat. no. 16) and Claude, are characteristically wild, rugged, and expressive of tempestuous emotion. After his training in Naples, Rosa spent virtually his entire career in Rome, except for a decade spent at the Medici court in Florence during the 1640s. In this period Rosa occupied the centre of a circle of poets and intellectuals, and his landscapes, previously populated by generically picturesque figures, became charged with a more serious expressive and philosophical content. Back in Rome after 1650, Rosa developed a number of new types of subject, often involving the macabre, but he became increasingly frustrated with the constraints of conventional systems of patronage. His rebellious personality, as well as his wildly dramatic landscapes, made him a figure of particular fascination to artists of the Romantic period of the late eighteenth and early nineteenth centuries.

Painted on a monumental scale, this picture and its companion, the *St John the Baptist Baptizing Christ in the Jordan* (cat. no. 20), are widely recognized as two of Rosa's very finest works. Each shows a

St John the Baptist Revealing Christ to the Disciples, 1656–57

Oil on canvas, 174 x 258 cm; 68.5 x 101.6 inches
Signed: SR
2969
Presented to Glasgow Museums in memory of John Young by his family, 1952

19

Salvator Rosa

St John the Baptist Revealing Christ to the Disciples

scene from the life of the Baptist; in this case, the subject is based on the passage in John 1:35–6, in which the saint indicated the walking figure of Jesus to two future disciples, traditionally identified as Peter and Andrew, with the words 'Behold the Lamb of God!'. The painter sets the scene in the wilderness, with Christ seen at the far left, and adds a third, eagerly attentive disciple.

According to Rosa's biographer Filippo Baldinucci (writing in the 1680s and 90s), the two pictures were painted for the Guadagni family of Florence. Recently discovered documents have confirmed that they were commissioned in November 1656 by Maria Acciauoli Guadagni, through the family agent in Rome, and that the painter received his final payment in November of the following year. Baldinucci mentions a number of other works by Rosa owned by the Guadagni, including two smaller landscapes, and some 90 drawings. It is likely that these had been commissioned during Rosa's period of residence in Florence in the 1640s by Maria's husband, the Marchese Tommaso Guadagni, who died in 1652. The choice of the Baptist as protagonist of the two large landscapes would have been made to honour him as patron saint of Florence.

Like Domenichino and Claude, Rosa uses the grandeur of nature to provide an appropriately heroic commentary on the biblical narrative, but unlike them evokes a scene that appears savage and primeval, with shattered tree trunks, shaggy foliage, and towering, jagged rocks. The placing of the foreground group of trees nevertheless effectively serves to emphasize the figure of the Baptist, while the tiny figure of Christ is situated at the base of the long descending diagonal formed by the rocks. Beyond, the glow of light above the horizon is suggestive of a new dawn breaking for mankind with the advent of Christianity. The painter's preparatory drawing (showing the figures in reverse) survives in the Fitzwilliam Museum, Cambridge (fig. 24).

Fig. 24
Salvator Rosa, *St John the Baptist Revealing Christ to the Disciples*, Fitzwilliam Museum, Cambridge

Together with its pendant, the picture remained in the Guadagni family palace in the Piazza Santo Spirito, Florence, for two centuries after they were painted, and they were still recorded there by John Ruskin in a letter to his father of 15 June 1845. His further mention of them in the following year in the second volume of *Modern Painters* must have helped draw the attention of British collectors to them. In May 1875, the former diplomat Sir James Hudson, who had retired to Florence, wrote to a friend to say that he had been trying to persuade the Foreign Secretary to acquire the 'Guadagni Rosas' for the nation: 'They are grand pictures, and ought to hang in our National Gallery in the same rooms as the Claudes and the Turners'. Funds, however, were not forthcoming, and two years later the paintings were acquired by the eminent Scottish chemist and industrialist James Young (1811–83) for his home at Kelly in the west of Scotland. Young separated the two when he died in 1883 by bequeathing them to his second son and his eldest daughter respectively, but they were reunited in 1952–53 when both sets of heirs of the following generation donated them to Glasgow Museums.

20 *Salvator Rosa* (1615–1673)

St John the Baptist Baptizing Christ in the Jordan, 1656–57

Like its companion piece, the *St John the Baptist Revealing Christ to the Disciples*, this painting was commissioned by the Florentine noblewoman Maria Acciauoli Guadagni in 1656, and was acquired for James Young from Palazzo Guadagni in Florence in 1877 (see cat. no. 19). The two paintings were separated when they were bequeathed to different children on his death in 1883, but were reunited in 1952–53, when they were given to Glasgow by two of his grandchildren.

The Baptism of Christ is described in all four gospels. Here Rosa shows other people preparing for baptism, and witnesses of the event, in the left foreground and right middleground. As in the companion picture, the holy figures hold their own against the massive crags and trees by their placing at the base of descending diagonals. Despite the absence of the customary supernatural accessories, such as ministering angels and the Dove of the Holy Spirit, the religious significance of the event is underscored by the restrained majesty of the landscape, which recedes by planes into a far distance. Although Rosa characteristically shows nature as wild and inhospitable, the mood of the picture, probably by way of deliberate contrast, is distinctly more tranquil than that of its companion-piece.

St John the Baptist Baptizing Christ in the Jordan, 1656–57

Oil on canvas, 173.7 x 259.5 cm; 68.4 x 102.2 inches

1656-57

Signed: SR

2987

Gifted to Glasgow Museums by Mrs Alice Thom, 1953

21 | *Carlo Dolci* (1616–1686)

Adoration of the Magi, c. 1633–34

Dolci is known to have painted at least four versions of this composition, in which the sumptuously dressed kings bring their gifts to the new-born Christ Child. The earliest of the four, now in the collection of the Duke of Marlborough at Blenheim Palace (Oxfordshire), probably painted in about 1632, was commissioned from the still very young artist by one of the greatest Italian patrons and collectors of the earlier seventeenth century, Prince (and later Cardinal) Leopoldo de' Medici, younger brother of the Grand Duke of Tuscany. The Blenheim picture is also the smallest of the series (71.1 x 55.8 cm/28 x 22 inches), and is even more refined than the others in its handling. The present, somewhat simplified version, like the other two (which also now happen to be in British collections), was presumably commissioned by some member of the Florentine nobility, in imitation of the prestigious original for Prince Leopoldo.

In his long and successful career at the Florentine court Dolci made a speciality of small-scale devotional works of this type, in which a painstakingly smooth and precise pictorial technique was combined with brightly contrasting colours, enamelled surfaces, and rich detail. Of obvious appeal to his patrons, apart from his astonishing technical brilliance, was his ability to infuse his devotional subjects with his own deep personal piety, expressing a sweet religiosity verging on the sentimental.

Adoration of the Magi, c. 1633–34
Oil on canvas, 129.6 x 101.7 cm; 51 x 40 inches
154
Archibald McLellan Collection, purchased 1856

22 | *Carlo Dolci* (1616–1686)

Salome, *c.* 1681–85

The story of the banquet of Herod, including the dance of his step-daughter and the beheading of John the Baptist, is recounted in the gospels of Matthew (14: 6–11) and Mark (6: 21–8). Salome – as Herod's beautiful step-daughter was traditionally named – is here shown in elaborate, richly textured contemporary dress, and holding the head of the Baptist on a dish, a trophy that she had demanded from the tetrarch on the instructions of her mother Herodias. The subject was frequently portrayed in seventeenth-century Italian painting, but as has often been observed, it is characteristic of Dolci's fastidious personality that he plays down its violent and gruesome aspects, and presents it in terms of courtly refinement. In this interpretation, for example, the patches of blood on the white cloth on which the decapitated head is lying are treated decoratively, almost as if they are embroidered. And Salome does not gloat over her trophy, but looks offstage as she slowly advances, as if to seek the approval of her parents. Indeed, it is possible to see her as an innocent pawn in the struggle of wills between Herod and Herodias.

Salome, *c.* 1681–85

Oil on canvas, 122.7 x 95.8 cm; 48.3 x 37.7 inches

656

Purchased by Glasgow Museums through JC Robinson, 1883

Like that of the youthful *Adoration of the Magi* (cat. no. 21) of half a century earlier, the composition is known in a number of other versions, in this case at least ten. The earliest, now lost, but recorded in an engraving, was painted for Marquis Pier Francesco Rinuccini, a member of the Florentine court. Another, painted for Sir John Finch, British consul in Florence from 1665 to 1670, was later given by its owner to King Charles II, and remains in the British Royal Collection. The patron of the present version is unknown, but by the mid eighteenth century it belonged to the banker Henry Hoare (1705–85), creator of the celebrated landscape garden at his seat of Stourhead, Wiltshire. The picture was purchased by Glasgow Museums at the Stourhead sale of 1883, on the advice of JC Robinson, Surveyor of the Queen's Pictures.

23 | *Francesco del Cairo* (1607–1665)

Death of Cleopatra, c. 1645–50

The subject, much favoured in seventeenth-century Italian painting, is based on the account of Cleopatra's death by Plutarch (44: 86). Faced with imminent defeat by the Roman army under Octavian, the Queen of Egypt committed suicide with the bite of an asp. In visualizing the scene, the painter exploits its full potential for combining violence with sensuality, showing the naked heroine swaying in her death agony, while the snake winds itself around her arm and attacks her left breast.

The Milanese Baroque painter Francesco del Cairo made something of a speciality of compositions showing tragic heroines in close-up and half-length, swooning, suffering or dying. This was a pictorial type he first developed in the mid 1630s, when serving as court painter to Victor Amadeus I, Duke of Savoy, in Turin. In the present work, however, the greater fleshiness and opulence of the nude, and the warmer and richer palette, suggest a somewhat later date, after a period spent at the papal capital of Rome.

Death of Cleopatra, c. 1645–50
Oil on canvas, 129 x 97 cm; 50.8 x 38.2 inches
134
Archibald McLellan Collection, purchased 1856

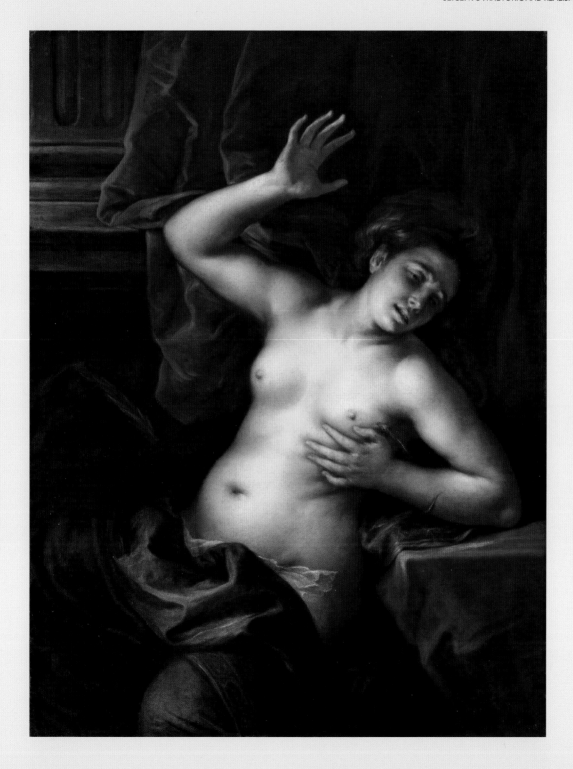

24

Unidentified Italian (?) Painter,
MID 17TH CENTURY

Vanitas, *c.* 1650/60 (?)

Until recently, this strange but fascinating picture was thought to be by the Spanish artist Antonio de Pereda (1608–78). In the nineteenth century it belonged to the pioneering scholar and collector of Spanish painting Sir William Stirling Maxwell, and formed part of the bequest by his granddaughter to the city of Glasgow in 1967. Pereda certainly specialized in paintings packed with still-life objects carrying an allegorical meaning; often, as here, referring to the brevity of human life and the vanity of all worldly pleasure. But careful comparison with the work of Pereda and of other artists working in Madrid suggests that the painting is not Spanish, but Italian. The artist, or even the local tradition to which he belonged, is not easy to identify. But a helpful clue is provided by the bronze figure group on the table, which represents the *Apollo and Cupid* of *c.* 1638 by the eminent Flemish-born, but Rome-based sculptor François Duquesnoy (1597–1643) (fig. 25).

That the unknown painter was also based in Rome is suggested by an item in the inventory of the collection of Cardinal Luigi Omodei (1656–1706): 'A Mary Magdalen leaning on her hands supported by a cushion on a small table by Mola, with an architectural perspective and a tablecloth thought to be by Fioravante. Seven by nine palms, with a gilded frame'.

Vanitas, *c.* 1650/60 (?)

Oil on canvas, 158.7 x 203.8 cm; 62.5 x 80.2 inches

PC.26

Gift of Dame Anne Maxwell Macdonald, 1967

24

Unidentified Italian (?) Painter, MID 17TH CENTURY

Vanitas

The female figure leaning her elbows on a cushion certainly corresponds to the traditional type of the Magdalen; there is a perspective view of architecture on the left; and the recorded dimensions (7 x 9 Roman palms = 156 x 201 cm/61.4 x 79.1 inches) are almost identical to those of the present work. Furthermore, the idea that the painting involved a collaboration between two artists – one responsible for the overall design and the figure, and the other for the lavish display of still-life detail (including Duquesnoy's bronze and the vase of flowers next to it, but also the various objects in the lower foreground) – is highly plausible. It was not uncommon for figure painters and specialists in still life to produce collaborative works in seventeenth-century Rome, and among these specialists Benedetto Fioravante was one of the most highly prized in the middle years of the century.

Cardinal Omodei is not likely to have commissioned the painting himself, but to have inherited it from his uncle of the same name, also a cardinal, and of exceptional importance as a patron of art. Among his commissions was an early version of Duquesnoy's group, a fact that could well explain its prominent inclusion on the table. Omodei Senior is also known as a patron of the leading Rome-based painter Pierfrancesco Mola (1612–1666), the artist named in the 1706 inventory as responsible for the figure of the Magdalen. A serious problem here, however, is the fact that the figure does not at all resemble the style of Mola. So is it possible that the compiler of the inventory made a mistake in naming Mola as the author? Or is Mola's own style obscured by that of his collaborator Fioravanti? Or does the item in the Omodei inventory not refer to the present picture after all?

Fig. 25
François Duquesnoy, *Apollo and Cupid*,
The Princely Collections, Vaduz-Wien, Liechtenstein

Even if not by Fioravanti, the still-life details are painted with
virtuosic skill. Particularly impressive is the magnificent
silver object in the central foreground, which has
sometimes been identified as a brazier, but probably
in fact represents an incense burner. While the general
meaning of the painting as a Vanitas is clear enough, the
significance of some of the details remains obscure. Mary
Magdalen is certainly included because having supposedly
lived a life of sinful vanity in her youth, much attached to
jewels and other worldly adornments, she renounced all
this for a life of penitence after her meeting with Christ.
While some of the various objects in the lower left may be
associated with female vanity, other elements seem to refer
to more general warnings against succumbing to an excess of
worldly pleasure, including that of smell (symbolized by the
opulent display of flowers, the beauty of which is notoriously
transient), sensual love (symbolized by Cupid), and objects of
luxury (including the bronze sculpture). The overall message of
the painting also seems to be that the way to cultivate the life of
the spirit is through the Christian religion – as opposed to the false
religion of paganism and Islam – as symbolized by several details in
the left background.

IV

Settecento :

THE AGE OF ELEGANCE

Settecento :

THE AGE OF ELEGANCE

The overall stylistic label usually applied to Italian painting of the eighteenth century (Settecento) is that of 'Late Baroque', which carries the implication, not altogether unjustified, that the principal stylistic trends of the eighteenth century represent continuations of those of the seventeenth. The period was largely frowned on by arbiters of taste in the mid to late nineteenth century. These included the influential museum director GF Waagen in Berlin, who still held the earlier seventeenth century in high esteem, but who categorized the eighteenth century as a period of 'Redecline'. It is somewhat surprising, therefore, that McLellan should have bought quite extensively in this area, and that he should have chosen not just from the generally more tolerated Venetian school, but also from the Roman. As a consequence, Glasgow possesses an impressive number of eighteenth-century Italian pictures, which besides showing an attractive variety of subjects and genres, are often of very high quality.

Detail from
Triumph of Galatea, c.1740–60

Andrea Casali

Oil on canvas

195

Archibald McLellan Collection, purchased 1856

Traditional religious subjects include Solimena's imposing *Virgin and Child* (cat. no. 27), and Trevisani's uncharacteristically intimate *Agony in the Garden* (cat. no. 28). Refreshingly unusual among Glasgow's Italian pictures, by contrast, are two sparkling and witty scenes from classical mythology, Pier Leone Ghezzi's *Purification of Aeneas* (cat. no. 29) and Andrea Casali's *Triumph of Galatea* (cat. no. 30), as well as a more severely moralizing subject from Roman history, Garzi's *Sacrifice of Marcus Curtius* (cat. no. 26), and a secular, probably political allegory by the Veronese Balestra, *Justice and Peace Embracing* (cat. no. 25). Venetian townscape is represented by a number of views after Canaletto, but more impressively by a luminous masterpiece by

Francesco Guardi, the *View of San Giorgio Maggiore* (cat. no. 33). A topographical, if delicately idealizing, landscape is represented by Paolo Anesi's *View of Ariccia* (cat. no. 32), a favourite haunt of British Grand Tourists. Finally, there are a number of purely imaginary, bucolic landscapes, by the Roman Locatelli (cat. no. 31) and by the Venice-based Zuccarelli (cat. no. 34). The last is another painter who enjoyed extraordinary success in his own lifetime, but whose reputation has still not yet fully recovered from a reaction that set in soon after *St John the Baptist Preaching* and four other pictures in Glasgow Museums were acquired by McLellan and Graham Gilbert in the 1830s and 40s. When his reputation does finally recover, it will be realized, as in the case of Salvator Rosa, that Glasgow possesses one of the finest group of paintings by Zuccarelli in any British collection.

Detail from **Agony in the Garden,** 1740

Francesco Trevisani (?)
Oil on copper
Inscribed on the reverse: Cve Trevis. Ro/ 1740 (Cavalier Trevisani in Roma, 1740)
145
Archibald McLellan Collection, purchased 1856

25 *Antonio Balestra* (1666–1740)

Justice and Peace Embracing, *c.* 1700

A native of Verona, Balestra was trained in Venice before spending the early 1690s in Rome. This Roman experience confirmed an early predisposition towards the light palette and formal clarity of his sixteenth-century predecessor Paolo Veronese. On his return to Venice in 1697, Balestra became the leading local representative of an academic classicism that stood apart from the loose brushwork and sensuous colour of his Venetian contemporaries. For the next two decades he remained mainly in Venice, but resettled in Verona after 1718. As a practitioner not just of altarpieces, but also of large-scale secular narratives, he came to the attention of a number of foreign patrons, notably the Elector of Mainz, for whom he painted a distinguished set of allegories in 1714.

The allegorical figure on the left of this painting is clearly identifiable as Peace by her traditional attribute of an olive branch; she is accompanied by a winged cupid, symbolizing Love. In the recent literature on the picture, the figure on the right has sometimes been called Power, and sometimes Concord, but according to the influential iconographic manual by Cesare Ripa, first published in 1593, the bundle of lictors' rods, combined with a crown, indicate rather that she is meant to be Justice. Ripa explains the bound rods as symbols of the judge's power to punish, and the crown as an indication of the regal status of Justice. The concept of Justice and Peace embracing in loving harmony carries obvious political connotations, which would have been equally appropriate for a public building or for a reception room in a private palace.

Balestra's paintings are not easy to date, and in the past this work has been seen as close to the allegories of 1714 for the Elector of Mainz. There exists, however, another version of the composition, evidently a copy, signed by the German painter Anton Negelein (fl. 1689–1740), and dated 1701. This suggests that the present work dates from *c.* 1700, soon after Balestra's return from Rome to Venice.

Justice and Peace Embracing, *c.* 1700

Oil on canvas, 106.8 x 140.3 cm; 42 x 55.2 inches
266
Archibald McLellan Collection, purchased 1856

26 — *Luigi Garzi* (1638–1721)

Sacrifice of Marcus Curtius, *c.* 1715–20

Born in Pistoia in Tuscany, Garzi was trained in Rome under Andrea Sacchi (1599–1661), and retained his base in the papal capital for the rest of his long career. By the 1670s he was much in demand as a painter of altarpieces and large-scale mural decorations. His style remained faithful to the classical principles of his master, and also shows the influence of the great French painter resident in Rome, Nicolas Poussin (1594–1665).

The subject of this painting is drawn from Livy's *History of Rome* (VII:6). In the year 362 BC a chasm suddenly opened in the Roman Forum, and soothsayers prophesied that it would be closed only when Rome's greatest treasure was sacrificed to it. A young nobleman, Marcus Curtius, recognizing that Rome had no greater treasure than the valour of her soldiers, rode fully armed into the chasm, causing it to close over him. In the picture this heroic act of self-sacrifice is witnessed by groups of citizens, and is set against a background of classicizing buildings meant to evoke the Forum in the fourth century BC.

The painting has been identified as a late work by Garzi of *c.* 1715–20, comparable in style and subject-matter to his *Cincinnatus at the Plough* at Holkham Hall (Norfolk, England). In both works, the moral severity of the subject matter has evidently inspired the painter to adopt the formal rigour of Poussin, with poses and gestures arranged on rectilinear diagonals, and stabilized by the firm grid of verticals and horizontals provided by the architecture. Likewise derived from Poussin is the somewhat forced rhetoric of the figures in the foreground.

Sacrifice of Marcus Curtius, c. 1715–20

Oil on canvas, 106 x 172 cm; 41.7 x 67.7 inches
900
William Kennedy Bequest, 1899

27 *Francesco Solimena* (1657–1747)

Virgin and Child, c. 1720–30

Solimena was the leading painter in Naples in the first half of the eighteenth century, and was highly productive as a painter of large-scale mural works, altarpieces and mythologies for the city's churches and palaces. The present work, in which the Christ Child holds a small bird, a traditional symbol of his future Passion, is characteristic of the painter's late style. Still typically Baroque are the undulating rhythms of the forms, the play of light and shade, and the fluent handling of paint. But all this is firmly stabilized by the pyramidal composition, with its base formed by the table in the lower foreground, lending the figure group an appropriate majesty.

Virgin and Child, c. 1720–30
Oil on canvas, 76.4 x 63.5 cm; 30.1 x 25 inches
143
Archibald McLellan Collection, purchased 1856

28 | *Francesco Trevisani (?)* (1656–1746)

Agony in the Garden, 1740

One of the leading painters of early eighteenth-century Rome, Trevisani was trained in Venice, but moved to the papal capital in about 1678. Like his predecessor there a century earlier, the Cavaliere d'Arpino (cat. no. 15), his success was rewarded with a papal knighthood. Throughout his long career his style alternated between the painterly freedom derived from his Venetian background, and the stricter classicism prevalent in Rome. The present work provides a devotional meditation on Christ's agony in the garden of Gethsemane, during the night before the Crucifixion. It seems to have been inspired in particular by the passage in Luke's gospel:

Father, if thou be willing, remove this cup from me: nevertheless not my will, but thine, be done. And there appeared an angel unto him from heaven, strengthening him. And being in agony he prayed more earnestly: and his sweat was as it were great drops of blood falling down to the ground. Luke 22:42–4

To help involve the thoughts and emotions of the pious viewer, the holy figures, illuminated by a supernatural light, are brought close to the picture plane, and the background is reduced to a single tree, a glimpse of distant mountains, and the night sky.

The inscription on the reverse would date the picture from close to the end of Trevisani's long career, when he was aged over 80. Its reliability should probably be accepted only with a certain caution, since his other works at this date, most of them monumental in scale, are much more sculptural in their handling. It could be argued, however, that for the small-scale intimacy of the *Agony* the master deliberately chose a looser, more pictorial handling.

Agony in the Garden, 1740

Oil on copper, 16 x 22.6 cm; 6.3 x 8.9 inches

Inscribed on the reverse: Cve Trevis. Ro/ 1740 (Cavalier Trevisani in Roma, 1740)

145

Archibald McLellan Collection, purchased 1856

29 *Pier Leone Ghezzi* (1674–1755)

The Purification of Aeneas in the River Numicius, *c.* 1725

Son and pupil of the painter Giuseppe Ghezzi (1634–1721), Pier Leone was born near Ascoli Piceno in the Marches, but spent his entire career in Rome, where he was also active as an antiquarian, collector, curator and musician. He undertook the customary range of large-scale public commissions, including fresco decorations, but more unusual was his specialization in paintings celebrating the lives of his contemporaries. He often introduced an element of anecdotal realism into these scenes of courtly ceremony, to be found in a more exaggerated form in his highly original and witty caricatures drawn in pen.

The subject here has sometimes been described as *Venus Giving Aeneas His Arms on the Future Site of Rome* (Virgil, *Aeneid,* 765f); in that case the bronzed figure on the left, wearing a crown and skirt of reeds, would be either the god of the River Tiber, or the god of the woods, Silvanus. More probably, however, the picture represents another episode from the life of Aeneas, as recounted in Ovid's *Metamorphoses*, XIV, 581f. The goddess Venus, having gained the approval of Jupiter to make her son Aeneas immortal, flew in her dove-drawn chariot to the point where the sacred stream Numicius enters the sea. There Aeneas bathed in the stream, washing away the mortal parts of his body, and having tasted a drink of nectar and ambrosia, became a god. One of Venus's cupids is accordingly seen holding the bowl of ambrosia, while two more play with his discarded armour. The river god would then be that of the Numicius.

The attribution to Ghezzi is relatively recent, and although it has not remained unchallenged it seems to be correct. Characteristic of the painter are the figure types, the light colour, the compositional rhythms, and above all the sense of humour, evident in the antics of the cherubs and in the caricature-like figure of the river god.

The Purification of Aeneas in the River Numicius, *c.* 1725

Oil on canvas, 97.7 x 135 cm; 38.5 x 53.1 inches

3233

Archibald McLellan Collection, purchased 1856

30 | *Andrea Casali* (1705–1784)

Triumph of Galatea, c. 1740–60

Trained in his native Rome under Sebastiano Conca (1684–1764) and then under Trevisani (cat. no. 28), Casali had a successful early career as a painter of mainly religious subjects before moving to England in 1740. There he lived for the next 25 years, producing large-scale historical and mythological canvases for grandees such as the Viscount Castlemaine at Wanstead (Essex), as well as a series of portraits for the Earl of Leicester at Holkham Hall (Norfolk). Between 1758 and 1760 he painted a cycle of mythologies at Asgill House, Richmond (Surrey), the house of Sir Charles Asgill, Lord Mayor of London. In the 1760s the painter exhibited regularly with the Society of Artists, but by 1768 he had returned to Rome.

The story of the sea-nymph Galatea, of her love for Acis, and of the giant Polyphemus's jealous anger, is recounted in Ovid's *Metamorphoses* (XIII: 750–897). According to this myth, when Polyphemus killed Acis with a boulder, Galatea made her lover immortal by transforming his blood into the river in Sicily that bears his name. In the painting she is seen being borne over the waves in her shell-chariot, surrounded by frolicking mermaids, tritons, nereids and cupids, while on the left Acis has already assumed the form of an aquatic deity, as he emerges from beneath the boulder that killed him. The representation of the nymph and the figures in her train is clearly indebted to the celebrated fresco by Raphael of c. 1512 in the Villa Farnesina, Rome, depicting the same subject, while at the same time translating it from a Renaissance idiom into one that may be described as exuberantly Rococo.

Previously attributed to Sebastiano Conca, the painting has only recently been recognized as the work of Casali. Particularly striking are its close resemblances of style and composition to Casali's *Birth of Venus* of 1758-60 in a private collection in Richmond (Surrey). The latter work, however, is considerably cruder in its draughtsmanship

Triumph of Galatea, *c.* 1740–60

Oil on canvas, 71.5 x 87.2 cm; 28.1 x 34.3 inches

195

Archibald McLellan Collection, purchased 1856

and execution; and if, as seems likely, it derives from the present picture, a likely date for this is some time earlier in the painter's career in England. With its pretty colours, rhythmically curving forms, and explicit eroticism, it would have been well calculated to decorate a fashionable interior and to delight an aristocratic patron.

31 | *Andrea Locatelli* (1695–1741)

Landscape with Fishermen by a Stream, *c.* 1730

Locatelli specialized in small-scale landscapes inspired by the countryside of the Roman Campagna, but usually showing ideal and invented, rather than actual, topography. During his short career he was much in demand at the papal court, and also by an international circle of aristocratic and royal patrons. Although following in the tradition of seventeenth-century painters of ideal classical landscapes such as Domenichino (cat. no. 16) and the French painter Claude, Locatelli's own work is lighter, prettier and more decorative than that of his predecessors, and the figures tend to be merely picturesque staffage rather than protagonists in any biblical or mythological narrative. This rural idyll is entirely characteristic of his work.

Landscape with Fishermen by a Stream, *c.* 1730
Oil on canvas (rectangular, with oval painted field), 47.8 x 39 cm; 18.8 x 15.4 inches
160
Archibald McLellan Collection, purchased 1856

32   *Paolo Anesi* (1697–1773)

View of Ariccia, c. 1760–65

A leading landscape painter in eighteenth-century Rome, Anesi was trained in the studio of Bernardino Fergioni (*c.* 1674–1738), where Andrea Locatelli (cat. no. 31) was a fellow-pupil. In 1729 and 1739 Anesi visited Florence, where he was briefly Zuccarelli's teacher (cat. no. 34). Although he specialized chiefly in ideal, imaginary landscapes, he also painted a number of topographical views of Rome and local beauty spots. This view of the small hilltop town of Ariccia, near Rome, is dominated by the domed church of Santa Maria dell'Assunzione, commissioned from Bernini in 1661 by Pope Alexander VII Chigi. To the left is the Chigi family palace, modernized by Bernini in the same year. In the eighteenth century the picturesque township was a favourite haunt of British Grand Tourists, and it was often depicted by local artists as well as by foreign visitors. Characteristic of Anesi, as well as of much of mid eighteenth-century Italian landscape painting in general, are the light colour range, the pale golden illumination, and the compositional rhythms based on gentle curves.

View of Ariccia, *c.* 1760–65

Oil on canvas, 59 x 85.3 cm; 23.2 x 33.6 inches

213

Archibald McLellan Collection, purchased 1856

33 *Francesco Guardi* (1712–1793)

View of San Giorgio Maggiore, *c.* 1760

Together with Canaletto (1697–1768), Guardi was the greatest Venetian view painter of the eighteenth century. This picture shows one of the most celebrated views in the lagoon city, with the imposing Benedictine church of San Giorgio Maggiore, built in the late sixteenth century from designs by Andrea Palladio, seen on its island across the water from St Mark's Square. The church is surrounded by its monastic buildings, and is flanked by its tall, slender bell-tower. While the subject and composition are clearly indebted to prototypes by Canaletto, the cursive rhythms, the contrasting patterns of light and shade, the luminous reflections, and the use of thick impasto, are all characteristic of Guardi's own distinctive vision of the topography of Venice. Compared with the work of the elder painter, Guardi laid much more emphasis on effects of fractured light and moist atmosphere, dissolving the solid shapes of buildings, and merging them with the surrounding water and sky.

The scale of the picture is relatively large for the painter, and he seems to have executed it as part of a group of four, possibly for one of the many aristocratic British visitors who included Venice in their Grand Tour of the sites of Italy. Although Guardi did not enjoy the international success of Canaletto in his lifetime, the impressionist and expressionist qualities of his art won him new admirers from the middle of the nineteenth century.

View of San Giorgio Maggiore, c. 1760

Oil on canvas, 72 x 120.6 cm; 28.3 x 47.5 inches

Signed: F. G. Fec

184

Archibald McLellan Collection, purchased 1856

34

Francesco Zuccarelli (1702–1788)

St John the Baptist Preaching, *c. 1740–45*

A Tuscan by birth, Zuccarelli spent most of his career in Venice, but also lived for nearly 20 years in London, becoming a founding member of the Royal Academy in 1768. He specialized in painting sweetly arcadian landscapes, characteristically bathed in soft pink and golden light, and these won him enormous success with patrons and collectors, both Venetian and British. Usually these landscapes were simply pastoral in content, and showed happy countryfolk with their flocks and herds. But occasionally, as here, he modified his usual recipe to introduce figures from a biblical or historical narrative.

In a composition based on one by the Dutch painter Philips Wouwerman (1619–68), now in the Gemäldegalerie, Dresden, Germany, which Zuccarelli would have known in the form of an engraving, John the Baptist preaches to his followers in an idyllic woodland glade, close to the River Jordan. The painter carefully follows the gospel account (Luke 3: 4–18) by arranging the saint's audience into three distinct groups – people, publicans, and soldiers – each of whom asked him what they should do to reform their lives.

St John the Baptist Preaching,
c. 1740–45
Oil on canvas, 67.3 x 51.7 cm;
26.5 x 20.4 inches
166
Archibald McLellan Collection,
purchased 1856

Zuccarelli's paintings are not usually easy to date, but it can be deduced that this work was painted shortly before 1746, since in that year a print after it was published. In a caption it is described as belonging to the Venetian engraver Carlo Orsolini (1704–1784), who presumably also commissioned it. Later in the eighteenth century the painting belonged to two successive British consuls in Venice, Joseph Smith and John Strange. It was brought to London by the latter, and was acquired by Archibald McLellan from the Bond Street dealer John Smith in 1846.

V

Ottocento :

PATRIOTISM AND GENRE

Ottocento:

PATRIOTISM AND GENRE

Detail from
A Painter and His Model, 1879

Pietro Aldi
Oil on panel
Signed and dated lower right:
Aldi-Roma/1879
2146
Bequeathed by John C. McIntyre,
1939

By the close of the eighteenth century, Italy had dominated European painting for half a millennium, but it now gave way to France, and most nineteenth-century Italian painting is undeniably provincial. In some ways this development is surprising and paradoxical, especially since the patriotic fervour aroused by the Risorgimento – the movement towards the political unification of the peninsula – had an energizing effect on the sister arts of literature and music. But no Italian painter emerged of a national stature remotely comparable with that of the poet and novelist Alessandro Manzoni (1785–1873) or the composer Giuseppe Verdi (1813–1901). Moreover, the abolition of the petty states of the ancien régime, and the widespread suppression of ecclesiastical institutions, resulted in the disappearance of most of the systems of art patronage that had been effective since the Renaissance period, without any corresponding growth of support by a wealthy middle class. It is true, nevertheless, that an inherited tradition of expertise was maintained by the local art academies, and at least on a technical level the quality of Italian painting in the nineteenth century remained high.

Thanks to the bequest by Mrs Cecilia Douglas in 1862, Glasgow Museums possesses probably the only two works in any British collection by the leading painter in early nineteenth-century Rome, Vincenzo Camuccini (cat. nos. 35, 36). Inspired by a high moral seriousness, and executed in a severely Neoclassical style to match, this pair of pictures can probably be interpreted as an early reflection of Italy's stirrings for political freedom. In this case, Mrs Douglas commissioned the pair herself, according to the

traditional system of art patronage still obtaining in the papal capital in the 1820s. Half a century later, however, most Italian painters were obliged to sell their work on the open market, through exhibitions or dealers, and consequently had to pay more attention to popular taste. Indicative of this situation is the fact that Glasgow's group of nine late nineteenth-century Italian paintings are all relatively small in scale, and in subject they consist of contemporary genre (cat. nos. 37, 38, 40) and historical genre (cat. no. 39), as well as orientalist genre and landscape. In style they continue to adhere to a pre-Impressionist realism, although in handling they vary considerably from the linear precision of Aldi's *A Painter and His Model* of 1879 (cat. no. 39) to Antonio Mancini's richly pictorial *The Sulky Boy* of 1875 (cat. no. 37).

Detail from **The Sulky Boy,** 1875
Antonio Mancini
Oil on canvas
Signed and dated upper right: Mancini, '75
2191
David Perry Bequest, 1940

35 | *Vincenzo Camuccini* (1771–1844)

Death of Julius Caesar. *c.* 1825–29

Camuccini was the leading exponent of Neoclassical painting in early nineteenth-century Rome. As a young man he was attracted to the classical severity of foreign painters such as Anton Raphael Mengs (German, 1728–79), Gavin Hamilton (Scottish, 1723–98) and Jacques-Louis David (French, 1748–1825), in reaction against the prevailing Late Baroque, and like them, he developed a style based on hard, clear draughtsmanship, straight lines, and simple colour. His artistic education also included a close study of the monuments of Ancient Rome, under the guidance of the eminent archaeologist Ennio Quirino Visconti (1751–1818). Camuccini enjoyed a highly successful career in the service of popes and eminent foreign visitors. This painting is one of at least two reduced versions of a monumental work, now in Naples, commissioned from Camuccini by the Earl-Bishop of Bristol and Derry in 1793. From the painter's own inventory compiled in 1833, it emerges that the Glasgow version was commissioned by Mrs Cecilia Douglas, a wealthy Scottish lady living in Rome, and was executed between about 1825 and 1829 for 200 Roman scudi (the currency of the papal states until 1866).

The representation of the murder of Julius Caesar closely follows the account in Plutarch's *Life of Brutus*. The scene is set in the Theatre of Pompey. Caesar, fallen onto one knee in the centre foreground, is surrounded by the knife-wielding assassins. The conspirator at the centre, towards whom Caesar looks and gestures, but who averts his eyes, is identifiable as Brutus. Conspicuously visible to his left, in an active, aggressive pose, is Cassius. Since, according to Plutarch, the conspirators had made sure that Mark Anthony (Caesar's loyal friend) was kept outside the hall, he may be the figure engaged in conversation at the far left. The male nude statue in the middleground is that of Pompey, at the base of which Caesar died. The statues in the niches on the back wall may be recognized as the tutelary divinities of Rome: Minerva, Jupiter, and Juno.

Death of Julius Caesar, *c.* 1825–29

Oil on canvas, 73.3 x 129.5 cm;
28.9 x 51 inches

318

Bequeathed by Mrs Cecilia Douglas
of Orbiston, 1862

It has been pointed out that Camuccini's conception of the story was informed not just by Plutarch, but also by a recent theatrical source, Vittorio Alfieri's *Bruto II* (1786), in which Brutus joins the conspiracy against Caesar, but does not actually strike him. The republican idealism of the subject was obviously highly topical in the early 1790s; and according to one of the painter's early biographers, Camuccini received detailed advice from the archaeologist Visconti on how to ensure that the subject was treated with the greatest possible accuracy. Despite the different pose of the right arm, the statue on the plinth is clearly based on a once very famous antique sculpture still in the Palazzo Spada, Rome, which in the eighteenth century was widely believed to represent Pompey, and indeed, to be the very one beneath which Caesar died. Similarly, the interior represents an archaeological reconstruction of the Theatre of Pompey, while the heads of Caesar, Brutus, Cassius and Mark Anthony are all modelled on classical busts and medals.

36 *Vincenzo Camuccini* (1771–1844)

Roman Women Offering Their Jewellery in Defence of the State, c. 1825–29

The subject, like the *Death of Caesar* (see cat. no. 35), was drawn from Plutarch *(Life of Camillus)*, and it was made particularly popular in the eighteenth century by its retelling by the Abbé Charles Rollin in his *Histoire Romaine* of 1738–48. In the early days of the Republic, the Roman general Marcus Furius Camillus made a vow to send one tenth of the plunder from the Etruscan city of Veii to the shrine of Apollo at Delphi. This was to be sent in the form of a golden bowl, and since the Romans had failed to take Veii, their patrician women nobly and patriotically donated their gold jewellery to the state to be melted down. Camuccini's version of the subject was preceded by at least three recent examples in pre- and post-revolutionary France.

Like the *Death of Caesar,* the *Roman Women* is a reduced version of a pre-existing larger work, and was commissioned by Mrs Cecilia Douglas of Orbiston. In this case the original (present whereabouts unknown) was painted in 1824 for the Duc de Blacas, formerly French ambassador to the Holy See, while the copy for Mrs Douglas, like another for the Duke of Poli, was painted immediately afterwards. The moralizing story, presumably chosen by the painter himself, the frieze-like figure composition, and the attention to archaeological detail, are all characteristic of Camuccini. Here, however, the painter takes more account than in the more rigorously Neoclassical *Death of Caesar* of sixteenth-century Italian models, such as the frescoes by Raphael in the Vatican Palace.

Roman Women Offering Their Jewellery in Defence of the State, c. 1825–29

Oil on canvas, 72.7 x 129.2 cm; 28.6 x 50.9 inches

319

Bequeathed by Mrs Cecilia Douglas of Orbiston, 1862

37 | *Antonio Mancini* (1852–1930)

The Sulky Boy, 1875

Born in Rome, Mancini studied in Naples from 1865 to 1873, and made two visits to Paris in the mid 1870s before settling in his native city in 1883. In his early career, as seen in the present work, he specialized in genre painting, employing a richly textured brushwork and thick impasto, influenced in part by Manet, but more especially by Velázquez, Rembrandt and other seventeenth-century masters. Here he shows a child from an evidently wealthy family in a domestic interior, surrounded by an opulent display of still life. Despite the strong characterization of the child, with his pouting expression, the painting may be interpreted as a genre picture rather than as a portrait of a particular person. In style and composition the painting is typical of Mancini's early work, in which he favoured relatively small figures, and emphasized richly patterned textiles, furniture, and other still-life objects, including dolls. Already by the 1880s he had adopted a lighter palette, and his handling of paint had become more rapid and more dilute. Later still he became a successful society portraitist and his work was championed in Britain by his friend, the American painter John Singer Sargent.

The Sulky Boy, 1875
Oil on canvas, 96 x 77.1 cm; 37.8 x 30.4 inches
Signed and dated upper right: Mancini, '75
2191
Bequeathed by David Perry, 1940

38 *Federico Andreotti* (1847–1930)

The Violin Teacher, c. 1875–90

Andreotti was a Florentine and trained at the Accademia di Belle Arti in Florence between 1861 and 1863. He was a painter of contemporary genre pictures, and later also specialized in historical scenes from the sixteenth and seventeenth centuries. Between 1879 and 1883 he exhibited at the Royal Academy in London, as well as at the Royal Glasgow Institute of the Fine Arts in 1890–91, and he enjoyed great success with British and American collectors. In this painting a violin teacher, perhaps a portrait of a real person, is seen next to his music stand. Legible at the top of the score is 'Lezione V' (Lesson 5). His gesture with his bow, his open mouth, and his look outwards all contribute to the effect of immediacy, as if he was addressing the spectator. The picture is characteristic of the type of earthy genre subject favoured by Andreotti in the earlier part of his career, but it is not possible to date the work more precisely.

The Violin Teacher, c. 1875–90

Oil on canvas, 31.3 x 25.7 cm; 12.3 x 10.1 inches
Signed (upper right, in red): F. Andreotti
2598
Bequeathed by Margaret H. Garroway, 1947

39 *Pietro Aldi* (1852–1888)

A Painter and His Model, 1879

Born near Grosseto in Tuscany, Aldi was trained at the Accademia di Belle Arti in Siena, where he chose to specialize in history painting. After a visit to Venice in 1874 to study the masters of the sixteenth century, he settled in Rome. He painted heroic and sentimental subjects from his own day, but was particularly attracted to medieval and Renaissance history. Among his most ambitious works are three frescoes in the Sala del Risorgimento in the Palazzo Pubblico in Siena, celebrating events from the life of King Vittore Emmanuele II. These were completed just one year before his early death at the age of 36.

It is not clear whether the title of this picture is Aldi's own. In any case, he almost certainly meant to portray the story of Florentine painter Filippo Lippi (*c.* 1406–69) declaring his love for the novice Lucrezia Buti as she posed for a painting of the Madonna. This anecdote, which derives from Vasari's *Life of Fra Filippo Lippi*, was very popular among French and Italian academic painters of the nineteenth century. Beginning, however, with Paul Delaroche and his *Filippo Lippi Falling in Love with His Model* of 1822, such painters customarily showed Lippi, as here, not as the middle-aged friar of Vasari's anecdote, but as a young gallant dressed in the height of contemporary fashion, and Lucrezia not as a responsive young woman only too keen to escape from her convent, but as a bashful nun torn between love and duty. Aldi took pains to set the scene in authentic early fifteenth-century surroundings, and he took as his architectural model the Sala di Balìa in the Palazzo Pubblico, Siena, with its frescoed upper walls, Gothic woodwork, and richly inlaid marble floor. The cavalcade represented in the upper right corresponds exactly to the fresco still to be seen in the room, the *Entry of Pope Alexander III into Rome*, executed by the Tuscan painter Spinello Aretino in *c.* 1407/08.

A Painter and His Model, 1879

Oil on mahogany panel,
27 x 20.2 cm; 10.6 x 8 inches

Signed and dated lower right:
Aldi-Roma/1879

2146

Bequeathed by John C. McIntyre,
1939

This picture, dated 1879, is a relatively early work, preceding Aldi's more ambitious history paintings of the 1880s, including in the Palazzo Pubblico itself. But already typical of his mature style is the attention to small detail and the meticulous finish.

40 *Luigi da Rios* (1844–1892)

Overlooking a Canal, Venice, 1886

This engaging scene shows women and children looking over the brick parapet of a Venetian canal, perhaps at some incident on the water off to the right. Behind them is a small square, and beyond that the belltower of a medieval church, clearly identifiable as that of San Niccolò dei Mendicoli, in the quarter of Dorsoduro, in the south-western corner of Venice. This has always been a poor neighbourhood, and the women, with their picturesque shawls, may represent the wives of boatmen or fishermen. The scene is clearly set in an actual spot, and the number of the house – 1021 – is visible above the doorway. But unfortunately this area of the city was developed for industry from the end of the nineteenth century onwards, and later, after the construction of the road bridge into Venice in the 1930s, as an area for car parking. Almost certainly the house no longer exists.

Luigi da Rios, who came from the Venetian mainland, studied as a painter in the Academy in Venice in the 1860s. His works included historical subjects, but he specialized above all in scenes from everyday life such as this one. These were aimed to appeal to foreign visitors to the city, and he exhibited regularly in Britain, including at the Royal Academy in London and at the Royal Glasgow Institute of the Fine Arts. This painting, which is signed and dated 1886, may be identical with one shown in Glasgow in 1889, with the simple title 'In Venice'.

Overlooking a Canal, Venice, 1886

Oil on canvas, 47.8 x 68.3 cm; 18.8 x 26.9 inches

Signed (lower right): L. Da Rios/Venezia, 1886

787

Beqeathed by Adam Teacher, 1898

Detail from **The Purification of Aeneas in the River Numicius**, c. 1725

Pier Leone Ghezzi

Oil on canvas

3233

Archibald McLellan Collection, purchased 1856

*Map of Italy
showing key locations*

Milan

Mantua

Venice

Padua

Ferrara

Bologna

Florence

Urbino

Siena

Assisi

CORSICA

Rome

Naples

SARDINIA

SICILY

Photographic Acknowledgements

All images are © CSG CIC Glasgow Museums Collection, unless otherwise acknowledged. All attempts have been made to contact copyright holders, but if any have been inadvertently omitted, please notify the publishers.

Fig. 11 Ken Currie, *The Bathers*, © Ken Currie, reproduced by kind permission of the artist.

Fig. 15 *Building Chronicle*, April 1857

Fig. 20 Reconstruction © Peter Humfrey

Fig. 21 © Professor Dr Max Seidel, reproduced by kind permission. Originally published in 'Signorelli um 1490', *Jahrbuch der Berliner Museen*, XXVI: 181–256; reprinted as 'Signorelli around the year 1490', in *Italian Art of the Middle Ages and Renaissance, I: Painting*, 2003, pp.645–707, Venice, Marsilio.

Fig. 22 © Accademia Carrara, Bergamo, inventory no. 162, Comune di Bergamo – Academia Carrara.

Fig. 23 Private Collection

Fig. 24 Salvator Rosa, *Landscape with Christ and St John the Baptist*, pen and sepia with grey wash, on paper, height 130mm x width 187mm, © Fitzwilliam Museum, Cambridge.

Fig. 25 François Duquesnoy, *Apollo and Cupid*, Sammlungen des Fürsten von und zu Liechtenstein, Vaduz-Wien.

Detail from **Vanitas**, *c.* 1650/60 (?)

Unidentified Italian (?) Painter

Oil on canvas

PC.26

Bequest of Dame Anne Maxwell Macdonald, 1967

Index (Numbers in italics refer to illustrations)

Index

Index

Index

Index

Index

of HEAVEN & EARTH

500 Years of Italian Painting from Glasgow Museums